Frontier Soldier

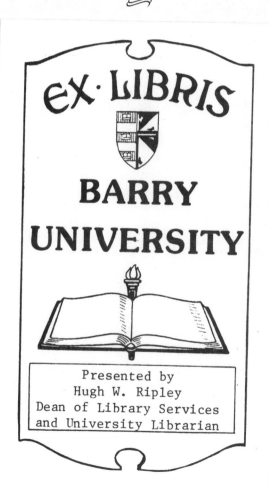

William F. Zimmer as photographed at Fort Wayne, Indiana, in 1881.

Frontier Soldier

∽

An Enlisted Man's Journal
of the Sioux and Nez Perce Campaigns, 1877

BY Private William F. Zimmer

EDITED AND ANNOTATED BY
Jerome A. Greene

MONTANA
HISTORICAL
SOCIETY
PRESS

Helena

Cover design by Kathryn Fehlig

Book design by Arrow Graphics, Missoula, Montana
Typeset in Bembo and Bernhard Roman

Printed by Thomson-Shore, Inc., Dexter, Michigan

© 1998 by Montana Historical Society Press,
P.O. Box 201201, Helena, Montana 59620-1201

98 99 00 01 02 03 04 05   9 8 7 6 5 4 3 2 1

Library of Congress Cataloging-in-Publication Data

Zimmer, William Frederick, 1874–1936.
    Frontier soldier : an enlisted man's journal of the Sioux and Nez
Perce Campaigns, 1877 / by William F. Zimmer ; edited and annotated by
Jerome A. Greene
    ISBN 0-917298-54-3 (casebound: alk. Paper), — ISBN 0-917298-55-1
(softcover: alk. Paper)
    1. Zimmer, William Frederick, 1847–1936—Diaries. 2. Nez Percé
Indians—Wars, 1877—Personal narratives, American. 3. Dakota Indians—
Wars, 1876—Personal narratives, American. 4. Soldiers—United States—
Biography. I. Greene, Jerome A. II. Title.
E83.877.Z55 1998
973.8'2—dc21   97–42962
                                                   CIP

Publication of this book was made possible
in part by funding provided by
the Montana Historical Society Foundation.

Contents

❧

Illustrations

～

Acknowledgments

I AM GRATEFUL TO Larry and Claire Sklenar, of Georgetown, South Carolina, to Claribel Zimmer Gottfried, of Cooper City, Florida, and to E. James Gottfried, of Fort Lauderdale, Florida, for making the Zimmer journal, as well as other pertinent family documents and photographs, available for this project. I must also thank Robert M. Utley, of Georgetown, Texas, for bringing these materials to my attention and for encouraging me to undertake their publication. Through the generosity of the Sklenar-Gottfried family, the original journal presently reposes in the Archives and Manuscripts Department, Harold B. Lee Library, Brigham Young University.

I must also thank the following individuals for their contributions to this work: Thomas R. Buecker, Crawford, Nebraska; Kermit D. Edmonds, Missoula Montana; Paul L. Hedren, O'Neill, Nebraska; Paul A. Hutton, Albuquerque, New Mexico; Ben F. (Colonel "Absaraka Ben") Irvin, Pablo, Montana; James Magera, Havre, Montana; Douglas C. McChristian, Torrington, Wyoming; Timothy P. McCleary, Hardin, Montana; John D. McDermott, Sheridan, Wyoming;

R. Eli Paul, Lincoln, Nebraska; Mardell Plainfeather, Crow Agency, Montana; Don G. Rickey, Evergreen, Colorado; Douglas D. Scott, Lincoln, Nebraska; Franklin G. Smith, El Paso, Texas; L. Clifford Soubier, Charles Town, West Virginia; Erwin N. Thompson, Golden, Colorado; Dr. James W. Wengert, Omaha, Nebraska; and Peter M. Wright, Oklahoma City, Oklahoma. Special thanks go to Charles E. Rankin, Martha Kohl, Glenda Bradshaw, and Kathryn Fehlig of the Montana Historical Society Press, for their assistance and valuable suggestions in helping prepare the Zimmer manuscript for publication.

Introduction

WHEN PRIVATE WILLIAM F. ZIMMER arrived on the Montana frontier in December 1876, it was to help reinforce troops that had lately experienced the trauma of defeat. Only six months earlier, Lieutenant Colonel George A. Custer had led more than 260 Seventh Cavalry soldiers to disaster and death along the Little Bighorn River in a bloody contest with Sioux and Northern Cheyenne Indians. Zimmer's arrival came in the wake of that event as the field troops prepared to rejuvenate their struggling campaign to force the warriors and their families onto a reservation in Dakota Territory. His unit, Company F, Second Cavalry, was stationed at Fort Ellis, close to the zone of operations, and would be expected to provide troops for any further army movements to counter the tribesmen.

The Custer debacle of June 25–26, 1876, transcended other army failures against the Indians in 1876. In March, soldiers from Fort Fetterman, Wyoming Territory, had struck a village along Powder River without success, and on June 17, Sioux and Cheyenne warriors had attacked Brigadier General George Crook's command at Rosebud Creek, Montana, forcing Crook to withdraw his troops from the area. Little Bighorn occurred eight days after Rosebud, and Second cavalrymen from Fort Ellis had been among those discovering Custer's dead. Thereafter, the army sent reinforcements into the area to support the stricken commands, and some successes against the tribesmen finally occurred. Campaigning in the fall and winter, Colonel Nelson A. Miles delivered the first victories, and it was with the expectation of more to come that the men of the Second Cavalry—Zimmer's regiment—prepared to take the field in March 1877. The "Montana Battalion" of the Second—so-called for the fact that its four companies (F, G, H, and L) had served together in Montana since 1869 (and would stay there until 1884)—would take an active part in the closing campaign of the Great Sioux War, including Miles's last major combat with the Sioux in the Lame Deer Fight and the ensuing movement of troops east to the environs of the Little Missouri River. The work of Zimmer's Company F would not end with the conclusion of the Sioux War, however, for those operations coincided with the arrival in Montana Territory of a large body of Nez Perce Indians, who were fleeing their Idaho Territory and Oregon homelands. Zimmer's Company F accompanied Colonel Miles's command into the Battle of the Bear's Paw Mountains, a climactic engagement that produced severe losses among both soldiers and Indians and led many of the Nez Perces to surrender.[1]

---

1. The disparate companies of the Second Cavalry had already played a major role in the events of the Great Sioux War by the time that Zimmer joined the Montana Battalion at Fort Ellis. Troops from that station had relieved the inhabitants of the trading post of Fort Pease, on the Yellowstone River opposite the mouth of the Bighorn, in February 1876. In the following months, Second Cavalry companies served with Crook at Powder River, Tongue River Heights, Rosebud Creek, and Slim Buttes. More troops from the Second had been with Terry and Colonel John Gibbon when the dead on Custer's field were discovered. In the fall of 1876,

Zimmer's involvement in the Great Sioux War and the Nez Perce conflict was of signal importance because of the journal that he prepared describing his daily activities and what he saw. As a soldier-observer in these campaigns, he was one of a few enlisted men who kept diaries or journals about their experiences. Zimmer's commentary covers the period from March 1 to December 31, 1877, and describes his company's involvement in the remaining operations against the Sioux and in the closing confrontation of the Nez Perce War. Beyond providing this chronicle of major historical significance, William Frederick Zimmer passed a normal life of otherwise unremarkable notice. He was born in Breslau, Germany, on March 4, 1847, and at age seven immigrated to Canada with his parents and a stepbrother. Zimmer's father died shortly thereafter of cholera and the remaining family members settled in rural Ohio, somewhere near Cleveland, where Zimmer apparently received his early education. At the outbreak of the Civil War, the fourteen-year-old traveled by train to Cincinnati. Unable to enlist because of his age, Zimmer seems to have worked first around Union mustering camps, then as a civilian ammunition wagon driver until he was old enough to enlist. During the waning days of the conflict, the eighteen year old went to Cleveland, and on March 6, 1865, enlisted for one year in the 191st Ohio Volunteer Infantry Regiment. At the time, he gave his occupation as "farmer," and was described in his papers as having blue eyes, light brown hair, and a fair

---

Crook's Powder River campaign again involved elements of the Second Cavalry. For a concise overview of the regiment's participation in the events of the Sioux and Nez Perce wars, see Joseph L. Lambert, *One Hundred Years with the Second Cavalry* (Fort Riley, Kansas: The Capper Printing Company, Inc., 1939), 118–48.

complexion; he stood five feet three inches tall. Zimmer was issued the requisite clothing, knapsack, haversack, and canteen, and transferred almost immediately to Company K of the 195th Ohio Infantry.

Details of Zimmer's Civil War service are unclear, but family records suggest that he accompanied Major General William T. Sherman's campaign to Atlanta and the sea that physically destroyed much of the Confederacy. If that is true, it must have occurred while he was a civilian worker before he enlisted. He was mustered out of the army on December 18, 1865, at Alexandria, Virginia. After his discharge, Zimmer apparently worked for ten years as a farmer and carpenter in Ohio until, on September 19, 1876, at age thirty, he enlisted at Cleveland in the Regular Army. It is uncertain what motivated him to sign up, but perhaps he was drawn by the surge of patriotism in the wake of the Little Bighorn that struck many young men; perhaps economic circumstances in rural Ohio dictated his decision. Regardless, assigned to Company F, Second Cavalry, he briefly underwent recruit training at St. Louis Barracks, Missouri, before starting for Fort Ellis, Montana Territory, where he arrived on December 11. Home to the Montana Battalion of the Second Cavalry, it was from Fort Ellis that Zimmer embarked on his participation in the Great Sioux War. It was during Zimmer's almost constant field service—between March 1, and December 31, 1877—that he composed the diary or journal that ultimately comprises this volume. It is unknown whether Zimmer kept further reminiscences of his army life, and he was discharged a sergeant of excellent character at Fort Custer, Montana Territory, on September 18, 1881, after fulfilling his five-year obligation.

Zimmer returned to Ohio, tried farming again, but on

June 1, 1888, reenlisted at Jefferson Barracks, Missouri, and rejoined Company F of the Second Cavalry, this time in the Department of the Columbia at Fort Walla Walla and Vancouver Barracks, Washington Territory. Presumably, his service at these posts was less exciting than that experienced in Montana during the Great Sioux War. While he quickly advanced in rank to corporal and sergeant, Zimmer never served out his term. Rheumatism and stiffness "due to increasing years" kept him from practicing cavalry drill, and the disability led to his discharge on June 24, 1890, at Fort Leavenworth, Kansas.[2]

Again, Zimmer returned to Ohio, this time settling in Cleveland, where he became a fireman. He later joined the Shaker church, but apparently left it and eventually went back into farming. Zimmer married late. In 1906, at age fifty-nine, he wed Nellie B. Garman, twenty years his junior, with whom he fathered two daughters, Margaret and Claribel. Plagued by failing health, Zimmer at age sixty-seven moved with his family to the town of Independence, outside Cleveland, supplementing his meager government pension selling chickens and honey and serving as a school custodian. Zimmer apparently never applied for the Civil War Campaign Badge or the Indian War Campaign Badge for which his service qualified him. In later years, however, he took pride in his veteran's status, participating in annual Memorial Day events with other Civil War veterans. He belonged to the G.A.R. (Grand Army of the Republic—a Civil War veterans' organization)

---

2. Details of Zimmer's military service are drawn from documents reflecting his enlistments in Record Group (RG) 94, Records of the Adjutant General's Office; and RG 15, Records of the Veterans Administration, File B855, in the National Archives, Washington, D.C., including appropriate microfilm publications.

William F. Zimmer with a neighbor child, ca. 1930. Zimmer wears the cavalry dress uniform and summer helmet issued to him during his second enlistment.

and was an honorary member of the Veterans of Foreign Wars. At the time of his death from heart disease on July 10, 1936, at age eighty-nine, Zimmer was the last Civil War veteran in Independence, and the community accorded him a dignified military funeral. He was buried in the dress uniform that he had worn during much of his service in the West.[3]

The Zimmer journal is an important document for several reasons. First, by its content it adds appreciatively to our knowledge about the army on the frontier, and particularly about military dynamics during the campaigning that followed the Battle of the Little Bighorn. It provides new accounts of the Lame Deer Fight and its aftermath, of the previously little-known, yet significant, Little Missouri campaign that concluded the Sioux War, and of the mission that went into Canada attempting to secure Sioux leader Sitting Bull's surrender to United States military authorities. In addition, Zimmer offers new information about the six-day Battle of the Bear's Paw Mountains, the climactic episode in the army's conflict with the so-called nontreaty Nez Perce Indians that brought on Chief Joseph's surrender. Second, the journal provides an enlisted man's perspective on events—an honest view of army life and routine from the rank and file—thereby contrasting with the often self-serving reports and reminiscences of military principals, usually officers, that have dominated our knowledge of

---

3. Information about Zimmer's civil life is from the following sources: "Comments by Mrs. Claribel (Zimmer) Gottfried" (Fall 1991), "Comments by his daughter Margaret (Zimmer) Wallhead [undated]," and Margaret Simon Wallhead to Mrs. William G. Miller, Independence, Ohio, October 6, 1978, in the possession of the Zimmer-Sklenar family; and various news clippings, ca. July 1936, in the Zimmer-Sklenar scrapbooks, maintained by the family.

these activities. In addition, Zimmer frequently elaborated editorially on subjects that piqued his interest, interjecting into his journal useful and sometimes humorous remarks about a variety of topics, such as Indian ethnology and military technology, and occasionally he offered commentary about the literature of the day that he read. His views about Indians probably typified those held by many enlisted soldiers about people so vastly different from themselves, and his sometimes deprecating remarks about them must be considered in that light. Zimmer's comments on Indians afford a window into the enlisted man's mindset, providing valuable insight into how the soldiers of the 1870s perceived their sometimes foes, sometimes allies.

Zimmer evinced concern for his natural environment, too, commenting on rivers, natural resources, and wildlife that he encountered while in the field. He also described the myriad communities that dotted Montana Territory during the waning heyday of the gold seekers. And although error or exaggeration of historical fact occasionally crept into his work, it remains the vital essence of Zimmer's enlisted man's memoir that constitutes its primary contribution.

In presenting Zimmer's journal for publication, the guiding objective has been to insure its clarity and to promote comprehension of its content without detracting from Zimmer's own unique style. Internal evidence suggests that the journal was transcribed from a diary or an earlier journal for presentation to an unidentified recipient, possibly a family member or friend. Although it is believed that such transcription occurred more or less contemporaneously with the events described, it is possible that in certain instances Zimmer called on his memory in transcribing his initial entries, thereby, perhaps, inadvertently embellishing some instances of fact.

Zimmer often wrote without regard to punctuation, and his entries were replete with misspellings. Again, for the sake of clarity, punctuation has been added sparingly, and only when necessary for comprehension. On the other hand, most of the spelling errors have been corrected to insure the journal's readability. Simple factual errors—wrong mileages or wrong dates recorded by Zimmer—have also been corrected with bracketed data in the text. Finally, the discrepancy between the closing date of the journal as evinced in Zimmer's title is unaccountable, since the journal ends three months earlier; perhaps it reflects but an unfulfilled intention.

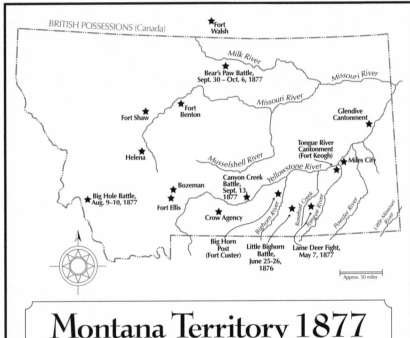

BRITISH POSSESSIONS (Canada)

★ Fort Walsh

Milk River

Bear's Paw Battle, Sept. 30 – Oct. 6, 1877

Missouri River

Missouri River

★ Fort Shaw

★ Fort Benton

Glendive Cantonment ★

★ Helena

Musselshell River

Tongue River Cantonment (Fort Keogh) ★

★ Miles City

★ Bozeman

Canyon Creek Battle, Sept. 13, 1877

Yellowstone River

Big Hole Battle, Aug. 9–10, 1877

★ Fort Ellis

★ Crow Agency

Bighorn River

Rosebud Creek

Tongue River

Powder River

Little Missouri River

Big Horn Post (Fort Custer)

Little Bighorn Battle, June 25-26, 1876

Lame Deer Fight, May 7, 1877

Approx. 50 miles

Montana Territory 1877

with sites referenced in Private William Zimmer's Journal

MAP BY JEROME A. GREENE AND KATHRYN FEHLIG

One Year's Life of a U.S. Cavalryman

〜

BOTH IN FORT AND OUT,
COMMENCING MARCH 1, 1877,
AND ENDING MARCH 1, 1878
[DECEMBER 31, 1877]

PART ONE

↬

March 1, 1877, to July 31, 1877
The Sioux Campaign

[ON MARCH 1,] Company F & G of the Montana Battalion of the 2nd Cavalry received orders to be ready for to move at the shortest time possible.

March 2nd.
Weather clear. Thermometer 10° below zero. After loading 20 days rations & such other things as we needed for camping, we were ready to start by 11 A.M. for the Crow Agency[1]

---

1. In 1875 the Crow Agency was erected on the Little Rosebud in Stillwater Valley, about eighteen miles from the Yellowstone River near present Absarokee, after a fire had destroyed a previous station on Mission Creek. Some three thousand Mountain and River Crows were assigned to the agency, a complex of buildings the purpose of which was to make the Indians remain peaceable and help them learn the practice of farming. The Crows in 1877 were by and large friendly to whites, and many of the Crow men had served as scouts for the various army commands operating in the region in 1876–77. For their history, see Frederick E. Hoxie, *Parading through History: The Making of the Crow Nation in America, 1805–1935* (Cambridge, England: Cambridge University Press, 1995).

As part of President Ulysses S. Grant's "Quaker Policy" toward the

on the Little Rosebud River 15 miles from the Yellowstone
River & 150 [approximately 110] from Fort Ellis,[2] our place
of starting. It has been reported that the Sioux Indians were
about to make a raid on the Crow Indians. This is the cause
of our being sent out in winter, to prevent them if possible.[3]
We traveled in the valley but a short distance (snow being 4
inches deep), when we commenced to ascend the mountains that divide us from the Yellowstone. As we ascended,

----

Indians, wherein various religious denominations controlled the agencies, the Methodists operated the Crow Agency. *Report of the Commissioner of Indian Affairs, 1877* (Washington, D.C.: Government Printing
Office, 1877), 132-34; Don Miller and Stan Cohen, *Military and Trading
Posts of Montana* (Missoula: Pictorial Histories Publishing Company,
1978), 26; *Crow Tribal Treaty Centennial Issue* (Crow Agency, Mont.: Crow
Tribe, 1968), 5, 17. In 1884 the Crow Agency was relocated to its present
site below Little Bighorn Battlefield National Monument.

2. Fort Ellis, established August 27, 1867, along the East Gallatin
River west of Bozeman, guarded emigrants to Montana Territory's
goldfields against attacks by Indians. Named for Colonel Augustus Van
Horn Ellis, killed at Gettysburg, Pennsylvania, in 1863, the fort was
abandoned by the army in 1886. Robert W. Frazer, *Forts of the West*
(Norman: University of Oklahoma Press, 1965), 80.

3. In his annual report, October 26, 1877, Major James S. Brisbin,
Second Cavalry, commanding Fort Ellis, wrote: "On the 3d of March,
1877, a large force of Sioux Indians was reported approaching the Crow
agency. The Crows at once fled up the valley of the Yellowstone, and I
sent Captain Tyler with F and G Companies, Second Cavalry, to protect
the agency. The march was a hard one, and most of the officers and many
of the men were rendered snow blind. After incredible toil and the en-
durance of every hardship, Captain Tyler reached the agency and took
post. He had traveled in the dead of winter over high mountains, through
deep snow, a distance of 110 miles, shoveling the road most of the way to
get his train along." *Report of the Secretary of War, 1877* (Washington, D.C.:
Government Printing Office, 1877), 552. The departure of Companies F
and G from Fort Ellis, ostensibly to protect the Crow Agency, simply
preceded a planned movement of the entire Second Cavalry battalion of
four companies to aid in the operations against the Lakota, or Western
Sioux, and Northern Cheyenne Indians, expected to resume that spring.
Bozeman Times, March 22, 1877. (See footnote 17.)

the snow increased in depth & our progress was very slow. We made, I think, 8 miles when our mules became tired, and the wagons were stuck in 4 feet of snow. Some of G Co. wagons being over a mile in the rear of the first ones, so they were obliged to go without tents for the night, it being dark already. We done nothing towards trying to get the wagons out. Besides, the cold began to increase, so we pitched our tents as best we could & turned in for the night.

March 3rd.
Ther. 20° below zero. Lots of the men froze their feet, ears & fingers in their bunks.⁴ It moderated some during the day. We helped the wagons up to the divide or summit, the distance of 5 miles, & returned to our old camp for the night. The snow was from 3 to 4 feet deep most of the way.

" 4th.
Ther. 25° below zero, yet we stood it better than last night, having fixed our tents better & fire was kept nearly all night. Yet some of the boys froze their faces. We made good time, it being nearly all down hill for the wagons. We are camped for the night amongst the foothills.

" 5th.
Not so cold last night. It snowed more or less all night. By 9 A.M. the wind was blowing a gale & we had hard work to keep our horses headed against it. By 12 m [meridian, or midday] we reached the Yellowstone bottoms, the wind had

---

4. Zimmer here meant "bedding" or "blankets" rather than "bunks," since the heavy wooden or iron barrack bedsteads would have remained at the post.

ceased blowing & the sun was shining beautiful. The river is about 300 yards wide & very strong & gravelly bottom[ed]. It's not very deep this time of year, yet the current is swift. This river is called by scientific men the swiftest in the world, taking in consideration the amount of water that flows down, & the 1000 miles in length. The average current in its whole length is 8 miles per hour.[5] We followed down the river to the mouth of Shields River (passing an Indian trading post on the way), & went in camp. Shields Riv is about 25 yards wide & very shallow now. We hobbled our horses out awhile to let them pick at the winter-killed grass, for they will not likely get any hay for a long while. There's very little snow here & in places now. By 6 P.M. it grew colder & commenced blowing & hailing.

Mar 6th.

The wind blew a perfect gale last night, upsetting & tearing tents & wagon covers. It's not below zero & the snow flies lively. We followed up Shields River about 1 mile then took to our right across a large knoll called Sheep Mountain, the wind blowing the snow fearful. By 12 M it stopped & by 4 P.M. commenced again. Here we went in camp one mile from the Yellowstone on a stream called Hot Spring Creek, or Hunters Hot Spring. We were ¾ of a mile from

---

5. For the natural history and ecology of the Yellowstone Basin and its environs, see Dennis H Knight, *Mountains and Plain: The Ecology of Wyoming Landscapes* (New Haven: Yale University Press, 1994), 67–107; and Lauren Brown, *Grasslands* (New York: Alfred A. Knopf, n.d.), 45–63. For a contemporary history of the region, see E. S. Topping, *The Chronicles of the Yellowstone* (1883; reprint, Minneapolis: Ross and Haines, Inc., 1968), and for a modern telling, see Mark H. Brown, *The Plainsmen of the Yellowstone: A History of the Yellowstone Basin* (New York: G. P. Putnam's Sons, 1961).

the spring & yet the water was more than lukewarm. Some of the boys went to the spring. There's a log hut built over it (for bathing purposes, I suppose) & the water just where it bubbles out is nearly scalding hot. It runs [in] a stream, 1 foot in diam. There was no wood on the stream & we were obliged to go back 1 mile with a team & bring some.

" *7th.*

It's still snowing & the snow is 2 feet deep but not very cold. We had some trouble with the train by getting off of the trail. Some upset & others broke some of their parts. By noon it stopped snowing, & at the ford of the Yellowstone [all was] ready to cross. The train went across all right, but when the company commenced to cross fun commenced for some, to see the horses dump their riders in the drink. A goodly number of both cos. fell in. But all wrongs were soon righted by the doctor's liberal introduction of the whiskey bottle (I think more would have got wet had they known that whiskey would be dealt out to the wet ones). We went but a little way further & went in camp. We are now on the south side of the Yellowstone. Some of the rear guard of our co. got some liquor of the trader at the ford & got in trouble. Mr. Q. got his ear broke by the corporal for refusing some duty & Mr. H. was riding his horse around like some Irish duke. He got tied up to a cottonwood tree for 3 hours to freeze sober.

March 8th.

This morning the ther. is 10° below zero. The snow is yet 2 feet deep. By 12 M we reached the Boulder River, the bottom of which is full of large boulders. It's a pretty clear stream about 100 feet wide & empties in the Yellowstone. We have been in sight of the Yellowstone all day. We had

no accident in crossing the Boulder, only the breaking of
one coupling pole. This evening we are camped on Deer
Creek & it's freezing very hard.

" 9th.
Last night was the coldest that any man in our outfit ever
put in. It was 35° below zero, more frozen feet & hands, &
nearly everyone froze either his chin or nose. I don't believe that Old Washington & party ever suffered more in
Valley Forge than did we. About 12 we reached Bridger
Creek. Here was a large camp of Crow Indians who were
scared away from the agency, & 3 miles below on the
Yellowstone is another large one. We had either to cross the
Yellowstone & recross [here] or [do the same at] Bridger
Mountain, so we took the latter. By this time the weather
had moderated a great deal & every one was warmed up by
the time we got the 12 wagons up the 2-mile hill, which
was very steep. 12 mules were put to each wagon, besides
the help of us. On top the country was perfectly flat, & the
snow was only 1 foot. We made several miles further, then
we were unable to find water & but little wood. We went
in camp & melted snow for coffee.

March 10th.
The weather has been quite mild. The country is like a
rolling prairie, with an occasional steep ravine, which caused
us some trouble & the breaking of a wheel of one of our
wagons. Its load was put on others & it left. Our dogs (of
which we have 3) killed a porcupine here, the first I ever
saw. The dogs were nearly as badly punished as the animal.
Some of our men are getting snow-blind. My eyes have felt
bad all day, as though I'd been standing over a smoky fire.

This evening we are camped on Stillwater River. It's much like Shields Riv, only more water & not so swift in current.

" *11th.*

It's been thawing all day. This morning 2 swing mules came near drowning while crossing Stillwater. 2 of the drivers were obliged to get in the river to untangle them. Rather a cold bath so early in the morning, but the doctor's bottle made things square again. A couple of hours brought us to the Little Rosebud Riv. In crossing this, our captain, whose name is Tyler,[6] got a bath. He is also snow-blind (my eyes have felt today as though I'd been hit in the eyes with a hard snowball). We followed the Rosebud up a few miles & came to the Agency & went in camp opposite from it at an early hour.

March 12th.

It's thawed most of the day & we have been covering the bottom of our tents with willows to keep us out of the water. Mc & Fr.,[7] both of our co., got hostile at each other,

---

6. A native of Maryland, George L. Tyler (1839–1881) had served as lieutenant of Maryland troops during the Civil War. Breveted captain for gallantry and meritorious service in the Battle of the Wilderness in Virginia, Tyler resigned from the volunteers in 1864. Less than two years later, he accepted a commission as captain in the Thirty-sixth U.S. Infantry, but went unassigned during reorganization of the army in 1869. Late in 1870 he was appointed to the Second Cavalry. Francis B. Heitman, comp., *Historical Register and Dictionary of the United States Army, from its Organization, September 29, 1789, to March 2, 1903*, 2 vols. (Washington, D.C.: Government Printing Office, 1903), 1:977.

7. Probably Private Samuel Fryer and Private James McNally or William D. McNeil, all of Company F. Muster Roll, Company F, Second Cavalry, June 30, 1877, to August 31, 1877. Regular Army Muster Rolls, Record Group 94, Records of the Adjutant General's Office, National Archives, Washington, D.C. (hereafter RG 94 RAMR, NA).

so they battered one another's eyes awhile & Mc squealed. At midday I was entirely [snow]blind. Our camp is overrun with Indians (they are camped all around us) and each one has a letter of introduction & they read as follows: "This is a good Indian, good warrior & guide, & any gift you may see fit to bestow on him in the shape of hard bread, coffee, sugar, or ammunition will be thankfully received." Signed by some one that never was dreamt of & perhaps the Red Devil had to give a robe to have it written.

" *13th.*

It has thawed fast all day, part of the time raining. Since our arrival at the agency the Indians have been coming back in large numbers. This thing of the Sioux moving on the agency was only a scare. They couldn't come if they wanted to, the snow is too deep yet in most of places. Besides, their ponies couldn't get enough to live on everywhere in winter. This is ration day for the Indians and they came flocking in in large number. These Indians seem to be very dissatisfied with their agent. They say he don't give them their allowance, that he don't give them anything but beef when they should have flour, coffee & sugar, as well.[8] I was at the agency this afternoon. There is 2 stores, one government & one private, 2 government warehouses, one large adobe house for the agent & doctor, & 10 small adobe houses occupied by halfbreeds or white men married to squaws, besides a blacksmith shop & school house. I understand that there's

---

8. For the Crows' treaty with the government in 1868, including specifics regarding annuities, see Charles J. Kappler, comp., ed., *Indian Affairs: Law and Treaties* (Washington, D.C.: Government Printing Office, 1904), 2:1008-11.

never any school or divine services held in it, yet some one
draws pay for school teaching, for the government allows a
teacher & a chaplain.[9] My eyes are a little better.

Mar 14th.

Weather warm & cloudy, my eyes are improving fast. Half
of the teams (which is six) were sent back to Ft. Ellis with
a small escort for rations & oats. I think it's nearly time, for
the agent will give us nothing but beef. There's about 1,000
warriors belonging to this agency, besides their families.
They have from one to five wives [and] they do all the
work, chop & tote the wood, or pack it on ponies, saddle &
unsaddle their lord's pony & put him with the rest of the
herd, in fact everything. When they move camp the squaws
have to do the packing & unpacking, drive the ponies &
look after the babies & dogs.[10] They have from 2 to 12
ponies & dogs by the 100. Our horses are commencing to
look poor, their oats have been cut down from 12 qts to 4

---

9. The Indian agent at this time was Dexter E. Clapp, soon to be
succeeded in July by George W. Frost. Conditions at the agency were
not good in 1876–77, when encroachers and nearby whiskey sellers
worked to distract the tribesmen from the government-sponsored ag-
ricultural programs. *Report of the Commissioner of Indian Affairs, 1876* (Washington, D.C.: Government Printing Office, 1876), 87-88. As Zimmer
noted, the school was a particular failure because, reported Agent Frost
in August 1877, "the compensation is so small that but few teachers of
ability . . . can be secured. It requires peculiar tact, patience, and energy
of character to be successful." *Report of the Commissioner of Indian Affairs,
1877* (Washington, D.C.: Government Printing Office, 1877), 134.

10. Contrary to Zimmer's observations, Crow women were not mere
drudges for their husbands. Women were active in many aspects of Crow
society. While they indeed tended to household duties, including the
manufacture of tepees and clothing and the preservation and storage of
essential foods, they also enjoyed considerable independence as teachers
of the young, medicine healers, participants in religious ceremonies,

because they are getting scarce & for grazing there's nothing. There's too much Indian stock about. Yesterday a team was sent after the broken wagon & they have just returned. The boys spend the days & evenings by playing cards (sometimes with Indians, who are very fond of gambling & when they get excited they will make very rash bets. I have heard of them, when playing with themselves, to gamble off their ponies & even their squaws), singing religious, sentimental & comic songs, reading, telling stories of their school boy days or their adventures & travels. One can find in the army all nationalities & from every state & territory in our Union.[11]

March 15th.
The forepart of the day was very fine. About noon there came a heavy wind & rain storm lasting two hours.

" *16th.*
The weather has been very warm for this time of year & the 2 feet of snow that were on the ground is fast disappearing

---

decision-makers regarding the family home, and occasionally as role-changers who assumed warrior status. These qualities contributed to insuring women's enjoyment of social status and spiritual achievement, reflecting the egalitarianism of Crow society. Rodney Frey, *The World of the Crow Indians: As Driftwood Lodges* (Norman: University of Oklahoma Press, 1987), 22-25; Hoxie, *Parading through History*, 45-46, 190-92. See particularly, Martha Harroun Foster, "Of Baggage and Bondage: Gender and Status among Hidatsa and Crow Women," *American Indian Culture and Research Journal*, 17 (no. 2, 1993), 121-52.

11. On the foreign- and native-born composition of the army in the late nineteenth century, see Edward M. Coffman, *The Old Army: A Portrait of the American Army in Peacetime, 1784–1898* (New York: Oxford University Press, 1986), 329-34; and Don Rickey, Jr., *Forty Miles a Day on Beans and Hay: The Enlisted Soldier Fighting the Indian Wars* (Norman: University of Oklahoma Press, 1963), chap. 2.

& the gray ground is coming in sight once more. My eyes are again well. (Those that were nearsighted or had weak eyes, were not troubled with snow-blindness. This seems strange.)

"*17th.*

Weather same as yesterday. We received 10 days rations & forage from the fort. It's St. Patrick's day & the boys are making the old camp ring with patriotic songs, such as "Wearing of the Green," "St. Patrick's Day Parade," &c., &c. I went over to the agency's shop to help repair the broken wagon. I heard a fearful howling like that of a lost dog, & on going out of the shop saw an Indian on a pony coming across the flats from whence it came. I soon learned that he had a child die & he had come to the agency for consolation. It's the custom with these Indians, at the time of the funeral, to hack their forehead and let the blood trickle down their face & there it remains until time takes it away. They wrap the dead in robes or blankets and suspend them in trees or on a scaffold made of poles to prevent wild animals from eating them. They always wrap up some trinkets & herbs for them to take along to the Happy Hunting Grounds. Some years ago, when bows & arrows were principally used instead of the Remington & Sharps improved rifle, they used to bury them with the warrior, & even kill all the ponies he owned under the tree or scaffold where he was buried.[12] As strong as an

---

12. The Crows traditionally wrapped their dead and placed them on four-poled burial scaffolds or in trees. Individual families mourned the loss of a member who died from natural causes by cropping their hair, chopping off finger joints, or gashing themselves with knives, as Zimmer explained. A man killed by enemy tribesmen, however, was mourned by the entire tribe. For rites and practices associated with death, see Robert H. Lowie, *The Crow Indians* (New York: Holt, Rinehart and Winston, 1935), 66-71.

Indian['s] belief is, he don't believe in sending many $50 rifles or ponies to that happy land. Perhaps he thinks there is better agents there than here & they will be better provided with chuck & they won't need any rifles or ponies there. (Perhaps you may think I've learned a good deal these few days we have camped amongst them, but you must remember this is only a duplicate & part of my whole summer's picking up.)[13]

March 18th.
This morning we had a wind & rain storm lasting one hour. These heavy thaws has raised the water greatly in the Rosebud. An Indian came in of [from] the Yellowstone & says she is booming.

March 19th.
The weather is fine this morning. Last night Gould[14] of our co. shot off 2 joints of his trigger finger while on guard. It's strange that so many trigger fingers get shot off & always accidental. This is the third one that I've known of. This afternoon we pulled up pins and moved over & up Stillwater 4 miles to get better picking for our horses. Just as we had finished putting up our tents, a norwester sprang up & she did howl, upsetting one of G co. big Sibley tents & tear[ing] ours badly. We had our tent just repaired when another storm came on, bringing snow with it. Neither one lasted more than half an hour.

---

13. Zimmer's parenthetical comment here indicates that he has copied his journal for an unidentified recipient, and that his remarks reflect insights gained throughout the course of the 1877 campaign.

14. Private Charles B. Gould, who enlisted September 16, 1876, at Boston, Massachusetts, returned to Fort Ellis, where he convalesced. Muster Roll, Company F, Second Cavalry, June 30, 1877, to August 31, 1877, RG 94, RAMR, NA.

" *20th.*

The weather has been very pleasant all day. One of G co. horses died last night. It's a wonder that more haven't died.

" *21th* [sic].

It's been very windy all day. Out of the wind it was very pleasant.

" *22nd.*

We had a shower last night. The weather today was as yesterday. Miller[15] of G co. refused duty this morning, so he was turned out with the herd and herded all day. 10 men & 3 officers went down to the Yellowstone to destroy some trader's liquors for selling to Indians.

" *23.*

Weather very fine. Our boys returned from the Yellowstone with several thousand rounds of ammunition & they spilled 5 barrels of whiskey. A mail carrier came from Ft. Ellis & brought us some mail & lots of reading. He reports that 7 mules were drowned & 2 wagons swept away out of those 6 teams that were sent back the other day & 2 men nearly lost their lives on account of the raise in the Yellowstone.

March 24th.

The weather remains windy.

------

15. This was Private Carl Miller, from Milwaukee, Wisconsin, who enlisted September 8, 1876. Muster Roll, Company G, Second Cavalry, June 30, 1877, to August 31, 1877, RG 94, RAMR, NA.

" *25th.*

The wind has ceased & the weather is very fine. About 300
Indians came & camped a little above & across Stillwater
from us. This evening they are making medicine. They call
religious worship medicine making, as well as Physics. They
make an awful noise about it, anyhow. I'll have to go & see
how it's done. The fine weather we have been having for
the last week has started the bunch grass, also the Black
Birch & willow buds. It's very strange how soon vegetation
starts in these valleys, when only a short distance in the
mountains one can see snow that lasts nearly till snow flies
again. (Here one can see some wonderful & beautiful sun-
sets. If Italy has prettier than these, she may well boast.)

" *26th.*

The weather continued fine. Another one of G co. horses
died last night. I have just returned from another medicine
making performance, although it's not over yet. They often
keep it up till 1 & 2 A.M. I'll try to explain it. Their doctor
is also their medicine man, or holy go [ghost?], who comes
out of his lodge (which they, the Indians, call tepee) &
gives a loud whoop to announce that services are about to
be indulged in (for it seems to me as though they consider
it as a kind of jubilee). They sit all around the inside of their
lodges or tepee & outside it the weather be warm, & commence a kind of a lingo, such as ha hi ho. They also bring in
the barking of the dog, the howling of the wolf, the bray-
ing of the donkey & once in a while a war whoop. This is
done by yelling as loud as they can & at the same time
patting their mouth with their hand. The squaws & children sit with their faces towards the tepee (let it be made of

canvas or skins) and thump it with their finger ends, keeping time to the other confusion. The only musical instrument they have is like a tamborine, only larger. This is brought in play by someone beating it with their fist or club of wood. This thing starts off very well at first, each lodge trying to keep in chord with the next. But they soon get mixed up. At one end of the village they will be yelling at the top of their voices, while Old Medicine is just getting to his fine work. This thing is kept up perhaps for 15 minutes when all is silent & the old man has something to say, & then they're off again. They have strong belief in their medicine making & they always go through with the performance in case they are going to start on some enterprise, let it be war, hunting, or on a horse stealing expedition. If they have been successful all is well. They never make medicine in praise, but if they had bad luck, their medicine wasn't strong enough & the next time they make medicine for any expedition they knock h--- out of the tom tom, which name they give their musical instrument.[16]

March 27th.
Weather cold. We had a heavy shower the fore part of last night. This morning we pulled up pins & moved to the

---

16. While Zimmer's observations of Crow ritualistic behavior reflect his ethnocentric insensitivity, that should not detract from the significance of his lay-person descriptions. The Crows were and are a very religious people, with their faith in an omnipresent Creator all-pervasive in their daily lives. For a comprehensive view of Crow religion and its many manifestations in Crow society, see Robert H. Lowie, *The Crow Indians* (New York: Holt, Rinehart and Winston, 1935), 237-326; Frey, *World of the Crow Indians*, 59ff; and Thomas Yellowtail, *Yellowtail, Crow Medicine Man and Sun Dance Chief: An Autobiography*, as told to Michael Oren Fitzgerald (Norman: University of Oklahoma Press, 1991), 66ff.

north side of the Yellowstone just opposite of Stillwater.[17]
We had no trouble in crossing this time. The scenery along
Stillwater are very nice. It has a narrow bottom in most of
places & the hills are generally high. They begin to look
quite green. We saw a very large flock of antelope on the
opposite side of Stillwater. These & a few elk on Bridger
Mountain is all the game we've seen since we left Ft. Ellis.

" *28th.*
The day has been cold. Yet the boys had a great time catching speckled, or mountain, trout (from 8 to 18 inches long),
and a greater time at eating them. This side of the river
there is a large bottom. [On] the other the hills come nearly
down to the water edge. They are not rocky but covered
with sod & dotted with groups of pine & cedar shrubbery.
The river side is covered with all sizes, shapes & colors of
stone. It only lacks the shells to give it the appearance of a
sea beach.

March 29th.
It has been cold & rainy all day & fishing was not so good,
although we caught some very large ones. They are indeed
the finest fish I ever ate.

---

17. The movement to the Yellowstone was prompted by orders
from Major Brisbin at Fort Ellis, who had been directed to proceed
with the Second Cavalry battalion to Tongue River Cantonment in
support of Colonel Nelson A. Miles in operations against the Lakotas
and Northern Cheyennes. Brisbin departed Ellis on March 25 with
Companies H and L. "I ordered Captain Tyler to move down to
Stillwater, with F and G Companies, and join me on the Yellowstone."
Brisbin to Assistant Adjutant General Department of Dakota (hereafter
AAGDD), October 26, 1877, in *Report of the Secretary of War, 1877*, 552.

" *30th.*

It rained all day. The paymaster came to us (with a few of H & L co. men, whose co. are on their way to join us) and paid us this afternoon.[18] Gambling is going on heavy. It is supposed that we will join Gen. Miles[19] as soon as Major Brisbin[20] gets here with the other two cos.

---

18. In 1877 army privates like Zimmer earned thirteen dollars per month and at remote garrisons like Fort Ellis were paid every two months by a traveling paymaster. See Rickey, *Forty Miles a Day on Beans and Hay*, 126-29.

19. Colonel (Brevet Major General) Nelson A. Miles (1839–1925) commanded the Fifth Infantry stationed at the Tongue River Cantonment along the Yellowstone. During the Civil War, Miles served as an officer of Massachusetts and New York volunteer infantry troops, and quickly rose in the esteem of his superiors. He fought at Fair Oaks, Virginia; Antietam, Maryland; and Fredericksburg and Chancellorsville, Virginia, receiving wounds as well as plaudits that brought rapid promotion. He also served in the Wilderness Campaign and was at Spotsylvania, Reams's Station, and Petersburg, all in Virginia. In 1864 Miles was appointed brigadier general of volunteers to command the First Division, Second Corps, Army of the Potomac, during the Appomattox Campaign, Virginia, and was promoted major general of volunteers after the conclusion of the war. Miles later served as custodian of former Confederate states president Jefferson Davis, but in the reorganization of the postwar army won appointment as colonel of the Fortieth Infantry. He married the niece of Commanding General William T. Sherman, a union that ultimately benefited him professionally. Miles emerged as a prominent Indian fighter following the Red River War (1874–75) on the southern plains and the Great Sioux War (1876–77) on the northern plains. He led campaigns against the Nez Perces (1877), the Bannocks (1878), and the Chiricahua Apaches (1886) before becoming commander of the Military Division of the Missouri. There he oversaw operations against the Sioux at Pine Ridge, South Dakota, in 1890–91 during suppression of the Ghost Dance. In 1895, Miles became commanding general, leading an unready force into the war with Spain three years later. He retired in 1903 following well-publicized policy disputes with presidents William McKinley and Theodore Roosevelt. He authored two autobiographies, *Personal Recollections and Observations of General Nelson A. Miles* (Chicago: Werner and Company, 1896) and *Serving the*

" *31st.*

During last night it was very cold & one of our horses died. In the morning it moderated & commenced snowing, which it kept up nearly all day.

April 1st.

It lacked but 15° of being down to zero last night. But the sun came out & the day ended quite warm.

Republic: Memoirs of the Civil and Military Life of Nelson A. Miles, Lieutenant-General, United States Army (New York: Harper and Brothers, 1911). A documentary study is in Brian C. Pohanka (ed.), *Nelson A. Miles: A Documentary Biography of His Military Career, 1861–1903* (Glendale, Calif.: Arthur H. Clark Company, 1985), while a synthesized study is in Robert Wooster, *Nelson A. Miles and the Twilight of the Frontier Army* (Lincoln: University of Nebraska Press, 1993). For Miles's operations against the Lakotas and Cheyennes, see Jerome A. Greene, *Yellowstone Command: Colonel Nelson A. Miles and the Great Sioux War, 1876–1877* (Lincoln: University of Nebraska Press, 1991).

20. James S. Brisbin (1837–1892), a Pennsylvania newspaper editor and publisher, entered the army in 1861 and served through most of the Civil War with the Sixth Cavalry. Brisbin rose to the rank of colonel of the Fifth U.S. Colored Cavalry and was appointed brigadier general of volunteers at the end of the conflict. He held numerous brevets, including those for brigadier and major general of volunteers for meritorious services during the war, including his performances at First Manassas and in the Peninsula Campaign in Virginia, and during the battles of Sabine Crossroads, Louisiana; Beverly Ford, Virginia; and Marion, Tennessee. Assigned to the Ninth Cavalry in 1866, Brisbin joined the Second Cavalry on the northern plains as major in 1868. He played a role in the opening phase of the Great Sioux War with the relief of the Fort Pease trading post, on the Yellowstone at the mouth of the Bighorn River. Appointed lieutenant colonel of the Ninth Cavalry in 1885, and colonel of the First Cavalry in 1889, Brisbin transferred to the Eighth Cavalry in 1891, less than a year before his death. Heitman, *Historical Register*, 1:246; William H. Powell, *Powell's Records of Living Officers of the United States Army* (Philadelphia: L. R. Hamersly and Company, 1890), 86; John M. Carroll and Byron Price, comps., *Roll Call on the Little Big Horn, 28 June 1876* (Fort Collins, Colo.: Old Army Press, 1974), 118.

Colonel Nelson A. Miles, as photographed at Fort Keogh in 1878.
Miles led the Yellowstone Command in 1876–1877.

" *2nd.*

A little snow fell last night. The weather remains cold. Two
Indians brought in a report that Parker, a government courier, while on his way with a dispatch for Gen. Miles,
drowned in trying to cross the Yellowstone 50 miles below
here. Two soldiers of H co. were with him, & they are continuing their journey alone. Y & T, [21] both of our co. had a
skirmish all to themselves, & several of the other boys got
into difficulty, all on account of the sutler arriving here
with some whiskey.

April 3rd.

It is very windy today, but out of the wind quite comfort-
able. Fishing is again good.

" *4th.*

The wind continues to blow hard. Co. H & L arrived at
I A.M. Major Brisbin will now be in command of the whole
battalion. [22]

" *5th.*

The wind has ceased blowing & it's quite warm again.

---

21. These privates are identified as John Youk and Edward Tilbert.
Youk (possibly "Yunk") had reenlisted in 1874 at Fort Ellis, while Tilbert
had joined the army in 1875 from Pittsburgh, Pennsylvania. Muster Roll,
Company F, Second Cavalry, June 30, 1877, to August 31, 1877, RG 94,
RAMR, NA. See also James Willert, comp., *After Little Bighorn: 1876 Cam-
paign Rosters* (La Mirada, Calif.: James Willert, Publisher, 1985), 14.

22. Also on April 4, Brisbin counciled with the Crow leaders in a
successful attempt to win the Indians' allegiance in the coming campaign against the Sioux. The Crows, after complaining about declining
amounts of annuities, nonetheless agreed to provide scouts for the army.
Bozeman Times, April 12, 1877.

" *6th.*

The weather is so warm that it's quite uncomfortable with the amount of clothing we have been having on. There's lots of duck & geese on the river & quite a number of the latter are getting shot daily.

" *7th.*

Last night there was a large wind storm & it's some cooler today. The whole command pulled pins & started down the river. We have now a train of 30 wagons. This evening our camp is on an old camping place known as the Lone Tree camping place. Here is a beautiful bottom & across the river is a lofty crag of rock where there is several eagles soaring about.

" *8th.*

Weather pleasant. We traveled all day in the bottoms, which are beautifully rich & level. The grass is up quite well in some places so that the horses are doing well with what oats they get. Pulling down tents is the program until we reach Gen. Miles. I don't think we will lay over much, except [if] storms stop our march. We are camped on the river bank.

April 9th.

Weather cloudy & some snow fell the fore part of the day. We kept down the valley all day & tonight we are camped on what is known as Baker's Battle Ground. Here Col. Baker had a fight with Indians in 1870 [1872].[23] He had our battal-

---

23. This fight occurred on August 14, 1872, near the mouth of Pryor Creek on the Yellowstone. Major Eugene M. Baker, commanding Companies F, G, H, and L, Second Cavalry, and C, E, G, and I, Seventh Infantry, was attacked in bivouac by several hundred Lakotas and Cheyennes.

ion of cavalry & 6 cos. of infantry. The Indians attacked the soldiers in the night, some 3000 & as soon as day light came they all lit out. There was but few killed on either side.

" *10th*.

Weather cool. We remained in camp until 12 M for we could but go so far or camp without water. This evening we saw about 30 Indians in the distance. Don't know of what relation they were. None of them came in our camp. The men on guard had orders to give the alarm if they saw any skulking about & the balance to fall in if any was given. We are camped on a high bluff near the river.

" *11th*.

Weather fine. The country has been rolling prairie and at times very broken. Indians in twos & threes have been seen

---

The troops were guarding surveyors of the Northern Pacific Railroad working in the Yellowstone Valley. One soldier under Baker's command was killed and three soldiers and one civilian were wounded, while Indian losses numbered two killed and ten wounded. *Record of Engagements with Hostile Indians within the Military Division of the Missouri from 1868 to 1882* (Washington, D.C.: Government Printing Office, 1882), 33; Topping, *Chronicles of the Yellowstone*, 92-93. Baker (1837–1884) was from New York. He graduated from the U.S. Military Academy in 1859. During the Civil War, Baker saw much combat, including that at Yorktown and Williamsburg, Virginia; South Mountain and Antietam, Maryland; and Winchester, Virginia, and won several brevets for gallantry. He operated in Louisiana after the war, but in 1866 was sent to the northern plains frontier. Baker registered a controversial victory over a village of Piegans in January 1870 in which many noncombatant tribesmen were killed. His devastating attack evoked a harsh media response in the East, where critics chastised the army for the killing of noncombatants and called for a reevaluation of military policy regarding Indians. (See part two, footnote 44). Heitman, *Historical Register*, 1:184; *Records of Living Officers of the United States Army* (Philadelphia: L. R. Hamersly and Company, 1884), 106-7.

all day. Our camp is near Porcupine Butte, on the Porcupine River. This stream is small & empties in the Yellowstone a few miles below. Porcupine Butte is a very large & high mound, and on its top arises a solid stone pillar of 20 ft high, & several in thickness, & at its base shrubbery & old crags of old trees are standing, gives it the appearance of an ancient ruin.

April 12th.

Weather remaining fine. The country has been a high rolling prairie. This afternoon a messenger [arrived] from Gen. Miles at Tongue River, saying that Lieut. Doane[24] was to return to the Crow Agency & enlist as many Indians as he could for a period of six months (that means business for the summer). This evening we are camped on the Yellowstone in a little valley where Custer in 1872 [1873] had a skirmish with Indians. Gen. Custer's[25] killed were [a] doctor, sutler & orderly.

---

24. Illinoisan Gustavus C. Doane (1840–1892) entered the Civil War as an enlisted man in the Massachusetts Cavalry. In 1864 he won appointment as first lieutenant of cavalry in the Mississippi Marine Brigade, in which unit he remained for the duration of the war. Mustered out in 1865, Doane joined the Second Cavalry as second lieutenant in 1868. He advanced to first lieutenant in 1871, and to captain in 1884. Doane became noted for his work with Indian scouts during the campaigns of the 1870s, as well as for his regional explorations. He died in Bozeman, Montana, at age fifty-one. Doane authored *Journals of Yellowstone Exploration of 1870*, and *Snake River Explorations of 1876–77*. Heitman, *Historical Register*, 1:375; Powell, *Records of Living Officers*, 177; Carroll and Price, *Roll Call*, 126. For a biography, see Orrin H. Bonney and Lorraine Bonney, *Battle Drums and Geysers: The Life and Journals of Lt. Gustavus Cheyney Doane, Soldier and Explorer of the Yellowstone and Snake River Regions* (Chicago: Swallow Press, 1970).

25. George A. Custer (1839–1876), from Ohio, graduated from West Point in 1861 just after the outbreak of the Civil War. Through the ensuing four years, he led cavalry units throughout the Virginia theater, rising to the grade of brigadier general of volunteers in 1863 and major general two years later. Custer fought at First Manassas, in the Peninsular

They were buried under a large cottonwood & their names cut in the bark, which is also dead now.

" *13th.*

Weather & country much the same as yesterday. This evening our camp is on the river again, but during the day the trail led us off several miles at times to shun bad places. Bears have been frequently along the river & tonight one was killed.

Campaign, at South Mountain, Brandy Station, Aldie, Gettysburg, the Wilderness, Yellow Tavern, Cold Harbor, Winchester, Five Forks, and Appomattox. After the Civil War, he participated in the occupation of Texas before becoming lieutenant colonel of the Seventh Cavalry. In the winter campaign against the southern plains tribes in 1868, he attacked a Cheyenne village along the Washita River in the Indian Territory. Later Custer campaigned against the tribesmen in the Texas panhandle. Following Reconstruction duty in Kentucky, he was assigned to Dakota Territory, where in 1873 he took part in the expedition escorting the Northern Pacific Railroad surveying party, during which he first engaged the northern Sioux. In 1874 he commanded the expedition to the Black Hills, which partly precipitated the Great Sioux War of 1876–77. In that conflict, Custer commanded the Seventh Cavalry at the Little Bighorn River, Montana Territory, where he and 267 officers and men perished at the hands of the Sioux and Northern Cheyennes. Biographies of Custer are numerous, but see especially, Robert M. Utley, *Cavalier in Buckskin: George Armstrong Custer and the Western Military Frontier* (Norman: University of Oklahoma Press, 1988).

The fight to which Zimmer refers occurred farther east, at the mouth of the Tongue River on August 4, 1873, during the Yellowstone Expedition. The regiment's veterinary surgeon, John Honsinger, and a sutler, Augustus Baliran, were ambushed and killed by the warriors. *Chronological List*, 55; Robert M. Utley, *Frontier Regulars: The United States Army and the Indian, 1866–1890* (New York: Macmillan Company, 1973), 242-43. Zimmer was closer to, but actually west of, the site of Custer's skirmish with the Sioux on August 11, 1873, opposite the mouth of the Bighorn River. For a treatment of the entire expedition, see Lawrence A. Frost, *Custer's 7th Cav and the Campaign of 1873* (El Segundo, Calif.: Upton and Sons, Publishers, 1986).

" *14th.*

Weather & country the same. We are camped on the Yellowstone again in a large bottom & grass is very good. So is cat fishing, but the beautiful trout are played out, as Bighorn River comes in just above & riles the water too much for them. More or less fishing has been done every evening so far & will likely continue [even] if the fish are not quite so good. In this bottom there is a large block house & a stockade around it called Fort Pease.[26] This was built by some trappers & it's been raided on by Indians several times. One year ago last winter some of our men went down to relieve 6 trappers that the Indians had surrounded.

April 15th.

Weather fine. Antelope plenty. Country level table land & our camp is on the river where all kinds of petrified articles are to be found in the bank. I'll name a few. Fish, crabs,

---

26. Fort Pease, named for trader and Crow Indian agent Fellows D. Pease, stood on the north bank of the Yellowstone a few miles below the mouth of the Bighorn River. Erected in 1875 by traders from Bozeman, the post was mostly used by wolf trappers, although its developers hoped it would become a strategic commercial point on the Yellowstone. Fort Pease consisted of a number of log huts joined by a palisade of cottonwood logs, in all occupying an area of about two hundred square feet. Early in 1876 the fort was besieged by Sioux warriors until troops of the Second Cavalry and Seventh Infantry, under Major James S. Brisbin, reached it from Fort Ellis on March 4. Of the forty-six occupants, the Indians had killed six and wounded eight. Thirteen others had escaped. With the relief, Fort Pease was precipitately abandoned. The action constituted the first military episode of the Great Sioux War of 1876–77. Edgar I. Stewart, "Major Brisbin's Relief of Fort Pease," in Paul L. Hedren, ed., *The Great Sioux War, 1876–77: The Best from Montana The Magazine of Western History* (Helena: Montana Historical Society Press, 1991), 115-21; Edgar I. Stewart, *Custer's Luck* (Norman: University of Oklahoma Press, 1955), 85-86.

snails, clamshells, & petrified wood in great abundance. The shore is lined with it & without much searching one can find some beautiful agates of all colors. Clear white are the commonest, then the milky or cloudy. But the prettiest are the moss agate & some beauties were found this evening.

" *16th.*

It rained hard this morning & we broke camp late & went but a few miles so as not to get in the bluffs to camp. What we did travel was in the river valley & it was very smooth and well sodded & grazing is very good tonight.

" *17th.*

Weather cold & disagreeable, sometimes sprinkling rain. It rained hard last night. We passed over some very rough country, but the worst was table land of a very poor soil. We passed a basin or pond on our way filled with a very small black duck. There must have been 10,000 of them. Game is very plenty, such as antelope, deer, sage hens & prairie chickens. Our camp is 2 miles from the Yellowstone on a creek. It empties in the river.

April 18th.

Weather fair, this after the sun came out hot. We were in the valley all day except once when we were going through a canyon. Quite pretty. Our camp is on the river again.

" *19th.*

Weather pleasant. We were in the valley all day. The grass is coming on fine.

" *20th.*

Weather the same as yesterday. We moved but a short distance down the valley in order to make a good camp where there was good grass for our [horses]. Oats are all gone & our horses are obliged to pick for a living.

" *21st.*

Had quite a snowstorm last night and it's still snowing. There's 4 inches this evening. We never left camp & it's quite cold.

" *22nd.*

It's very cold, snowed some during the day. We didn't go far. Camped on the river.

" *23rd.*

Weather mild. The country [is] high table land. (A mountain sheep was shot, & the lamb caught after the mother was dead.) We reached the mouth of Tongue River at 2 P.M., only the river is on the south bank. Here we went in camp.

" *24th.*

Weather very pleasant & the snow is all gone. Laid in camp all day.

" *25th.*

Weather fine. There is the whole of Miles's regiment (which is the 5th Infantry) & 4 co. of the 22nd Inft over in Tongue River Post.[27] Some are in log structures with dirt roofs &

---

27. Construction of Tongue River Cantonment began in late August 1876, following Lieutenant General Philip H. Sheridan's decision to keep troops along the Yellowstone through the winter of 1876–77. The

some in tents. Our boys went over & played Miles's boys a game of base ball & beat them badly. There is a flat bottom boat here used as a ferry across the Yellowstone & it's worked by mules.

April 26th.

Weather pleasant. At one P.M. we broke camp & crossed the river & went in camp on the bank of Tongue River one mile from the post.

" 27th.

Weather fine. Moved 1 mile further up the river for better grass. The horses are getting corn.

" 28th.

Weather fine. Major Brisbin started for Fort Ellis to day, his health being bad. Capt. Ball[28] of M Co. is now in command of our battalion.

---

occupation was intended to check movements of the Teton Sioux and Northern Cheyenne Indians following their success against Custer at the Little Bighorn. The cantonment was erected immediately west of the mouth of the Tongue on the Yellowstone. Its buildings—barracks, officer quarters, and warehouses—consisted of cottonwood logs set on ends in trenches and chinked with mud. Roofs were made of wood poles laid horizontally and covered with mud. The cantonment lasted until summer 1877, when more substantial accomodations were raised to the west of the Tongue River post, later known as Fort Keogh. It was from the rude Tongue River Cantonment that Miles and his Fifth and Twenty-second infantrymen conducted the campaigns in the fall, winter, and spring of 1876–77 that largely ended the Great Sioux War. Greene, *Yellowstone Command*, 57, 73.

28. Edward Ball (ca. 1823–1884) of Pennsylvania, enlisted under the name David Rey in the Fourth Infantry in 1844 and served until discharged in 1849. From 1850 to 1861, Ball served with the First Dragoons. Commissioned after the start of the Civil War, Ball transferred from the

Key to Officers' Quarters

No. 1— Commanding Officer
No. 2— Field Officer (not built)
No. 3— Capts. Butler, Bowen & Long
No. X— Baldwin & Baird temporarily (unfin.)
No. 4— Capts. Bennett & Hargous

No. 5— Drs. Tilton & Van Eman
No. 6— Unfinished
No. 7— McDonald & Bailey
No. 8— Field Officers (not built)
No. 9— Casey & Ewers

No. 10— Pope & one set vacant
No. 11— Maus & Carter
No. 12— Snyder & Randall
No. 13— Not built
No. 14— Rousseau & Post HQ

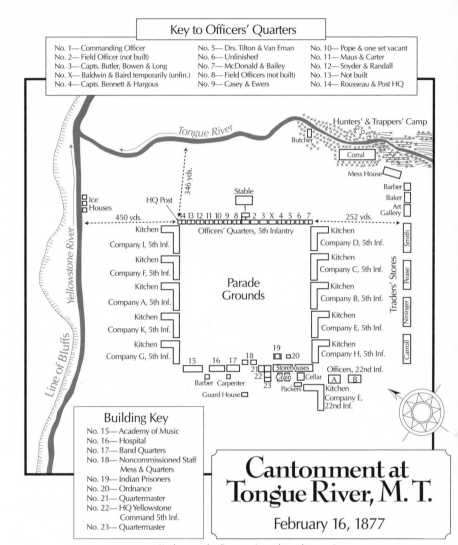

Tongue River
Hunters' & Trappers' Camp
Butcher
Corral
Mess House
346 yds.
Ice Houses
HQ Post
Stable
1
Barber
Baker
Art Gallery
450 yds.
14 13 12 11 10 9 8 2 3 X 4 5 6 7
252 yds.
Kitchen
Officers' Quarters, 5th Infantry
Kitchen
Company I, 5th Inf.
Company D, 5th Inf.
Kitchen
Kitchen
Company F, 5th Inf.
Company C, 5th Inf.
Kitchen
Kitchen
Company A, 5th Inf.
Parade Grounds
Company B, 5th Inf.
Kitchen
Kitchen
Company K, 5th Inf.
Company E, 5th Inf.
Kitchen
Kitchen
Company G, 5th Inf.
19
20
Company H, 5th Inf.
15   16   17   18
21
Storehouses
Officers, 22nd Inf.
22
Grain   Cellar
A   B
Barber Carpenter
23
Packers
Kitchen
Guard House
Company E, 22nd Inf.
Yellowstone River
Line of Bluffs
Traders' Stores
Smith Pease Ninninger Carroll

Building Key

No. 15— Academy of Music
No. 16— Hospital
No. 17— Band Quarters
No. 18— Noncommissioned Staff Mess & Quarters
No. 19— Indian Prisoners
No. 20— Ordnance
No. 21— Quartermaster
No. 22— HQ Yellowstone Command 5th Inf.
No. 23— Quartermaster

Cantonment at Tongue River, M. T.

February 16, 1877

Not drawn to scale—distances to rivers and to storehouses as given
Adapted from plat in Entry 107, Part III, Box 2, Record Group 393, National Archives

" *29th.*

Weather continues fine. We are remaining in our old camp.

" *30th.*

Weather fine. We were inspected by Gen. Miles this afternoon.

May 1st.

Weather quite cold. This morning we turned in our big tents & stoves & drew the small shelter tent. Soon after we broke camp & started up Tongue River.[29] 6 co. of infantry are with us. We have also two large trains, one of mules & one of oxen. The river valley is very narrow & we were obliged to cross & recross the river several times to avoid hills. The water is shallow & crossing is good. The river banks are well lined with cottonwood. There is also lots of coal sticking out of the bank.

Twelfth Infantry to the Second Cavalry, emerging from the war with the rank of captain. He remained on the frontier with the Second Cavalry until his promotion to major, Seventh Cavalry, in 1880. Ball retired from the army in April 1884, and died six months later in Santa Barbara, California. Heitman, *Historical Register*, 1:187; *Records of Living Officers of the United States Army*, 167; Carroll and Price, *Roll Call*, 116.

29. Zimmer's battalion joined Colonel Miles's command for what became the last major episode of the Great Sioux War. In March, the fruits of Miles's campaigning through the winter began to be realized with the surrender of many of the Indians at Tongue River Cantonment as well as at the agencies in Dakota Territory and Nebraska. Sitting Bull and his followers had taken refuge in Canada. By May, only a body of Minneconjou Sioux led by Chief Lame Deer remained afield in the Rosebud country south of the Yellowstone, and Miles determined to seek them out and force their surrender. Miles departed the cantonment on May 1, his command of the Second Cavalry, Fifth Infantry, and Twenty-second Infantry troops numbering approximately 450 officers and men, besides Indian and white scouts. Greene, *Yellowstone Command*, 201–3.

" *2nd.*

Weather fine. Continued to follow the river. There's some scrubby ash mixed with the cottonwood today. The first I've seen [since] I left the states, in fact the first hard wood of any kind. Grazing is very good. No game of any kind except wolves & they are very plenty. They howl every night.

May 3d.

Weather warm. The valley is the same as the last 2 days. The grass is getting quite large. It's as forward here now as it is in Ohio at this date in June. This evening while on guard we found a wild goose nest in the hollow crotch of a tree 12 feet from the ground. The eggs were bad. This seems strange, but they do build away up from the water. I have seen the geese on the Yellowstone sitting in rocky crags 50 feet from the ground & nearly ½ a mile from the river. I can't see how they get the young ones down without breaking their necks. This goose story would seem rather strange to eastern people.

" *4th.*

Weather warm. Had some rain last night. The river valley is becoming less & the country is becoming very rough & crossing the river is very common. We only crossed 10 times today. Early flowers are very plenty, different to any I ever saw in the east. Some are extremely beautiful. This evening we are camped where Gen. Miles had a skirmish with Sitting Bull[30] (by what I've learned, Miles got the worst).

---

30. The engagement that Zimmer references was the Battle of Wolf Mountains, January 8, 1877, against warriors from the camp of Crazy Horse, not Sitting Bull. Far more than a skirmish, the conflict began when the Indians attacked Miles's morning bivouac, then lasted several

" *5th.*

It rained all night & up to 12 m when it cleared off & the sun came out beautiful. We went but a few miles when the country became so rough that it was difficult to get the train along. We went in camp. Here we packed 17 mules for each co. & by 2 P.M. we were ready for a start. 3 of the infantry co. remained with the trains and the other 3 followed up in the rear. We are to make for an Indian camp somewhere in the neighborhood of the Rosebud (this is not the Rosebud River that the Crow Agency is on).[31] By 6 P.M. we reached the Rosebud, a very narrow & crooked stream. The banks are thickly covered with ash & willow & the banks are so steep that crossing is very difficult, besides it's full of quick sand. We followed up the river a short distance (by this time it was pitch dark, but still we kept on our way), then turned up to our right amongst the hills towards the [Little] Big Horn River. We never halted till 5 A.M. the morning of the 6th.

May 6th.

Weather pleasant. After the halt we fed our horses an extra dose & had breakfast. Then the scouts were sent out, of which we had 4, 2 halfbreeds & 2 Indians. In an hour's time they were back & soon after we were off again up a small

---

hours until blizzard conditions obscured the vision of the belligerents, and the Sioux and Northern Cheyennes withdrew up the valley. The engagement proved to be a victory for Miles and was significant in influencing the Indians to give themselves up in the spring at the Tongue River Cantonment and the Nebraska agencies. Crazy Horse surrendered at Camp Robinson, Nebraska, on May 6, 1877. Ibid., 147–200.

31. Zimmer's parenthetical reference is to Rosebud Creek near the Crow Agency in 1877, near the present town of Absarokee, Montana.

stream with a beautiful bottom & nicely sloping hills covered with green grass & shrubbery (the creek has all kinds of wild fruit on it, such as plums, currants, cherries, gooseberries & strawberries, & they are all in full bloom, giving the air a beautiful smell. Also another lot of new flowers are putting in their appearance). We hadn't gone far before we came to an Indian camping place, it having been deserted only a few days before. This is the place where they were camped when the scouts brought the news of their whereabouts to Gen. Miles (I had forgotten to state that Gen. Miles was with us). As the birds had flown, all we had to do was to follow their trail, which we did. It led across some of the highest points between us & the Rosebud in a circuitous route. On one of these high points the snow was falling, and below (it being about midday) it was warm enough for to go in one's shirt sleeves. From here we could see a great ways & oh, how beautiful & grand everything looked, we being amongst the clouds, & then to look down on everything in sunshine while snow was flying about us. It made things in the valley appear still grander. We stayed here just long enough to rest a little, for it was an awful job for the pack mules to reach to top. Some places they had to be helped to prevent them from falling & rolling down again. Our descent was nearly as slow as our ascent, for the trail was very rough & faint, they having scattered to get better roosts for their ponies, as they are heavily loaded with[out] a doubt. As soon as we reached a stream of water, & that wasn't till 2 P.M., we went in camp, ate supper & rested 2 hours. Here we left our packs & animals in charge of the infantry, they having just arrived by a near cut, as it was unnecessary for all of us to follow the trail. (One of the scouts was sent back to find the infantry for we had not seen them since yesterday. All we knew was that they were on our trail. As soon as the course of the Indian trail was decided on [the scout went to find them] & bring them up a nearer route if possible, which was done, as I stated on the other side [previous page of diary].) As I said before, we left all the packs except 2 for each co. loaded with ammunition, & by 4 we were on our way again. We traveled till 8 P.M. Then we laid down, strict orders being given not to start any fires or even strike a match.

May 7th.

At 2 A.M. we were awakened (but not with the bugle) & ordered to saddle. In half an hour we were on our way. It being totally dark, the scouts would give a little whistle so that we could follow them. We rode on in silence as though we were going to a midnight funeral. As soon as it became light enough for to know one man from another we halted, being on the Rosebud again. The captains of each co. told their men that we were about to attack an Indian camp & for all to stick together & fight like brave men, for the least signs of weakness might give the Indians the day & the result would be another Custer massacre. Orders were given to take all of our ammunition out of our saddlebags (of which we had 100 [rounds]) & fill our belts, the balance put in our pockets. After taking off our greatcoats, orders were given to [ride] forward at a brisk trot (finding the ammunition packs couldn't keep up, a few men out of each co. was left back with them) & shortly in a gallop. We had gone about 3 miles when we could see the lodges. We had left the Rosebud and we were going up a crooked stream which we had to cross several times, & the crossing was bad on account of quick sand. It was intended for H Co. to

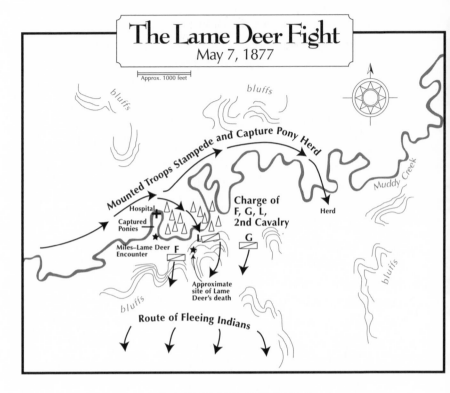

The Lame Deer Fight
May 7, 1877

Approx. 1000 feet

bluffs

bluffs

Mounted Troops Stampede and Capture Pony Herd

Hospital

Captured Ponies

Charge of F, G, L, 2nd Cavalry

Herd

Miles–Lame Deer Encounter

F

L

G

Approximate site of Lame Deer's death

bluffs

bluffs

Muddy Creek

Route of Fleeing Indians

MAP BY JEROME A. GREENE AND KATHRYN FEHLIG

charge the left of the camp & F Co. the right, while G & L followed in the rear to make the second charge, but as the lay of the ground wouldn't allow it, H & F Cos. were on the same side of the stream at times. About a 1000 yards from the camp H & F Co. set up a yell & started off at a break neck speed. About this time the bank on our side of the stream came down so close that we were obliged to cross & recross. This gave H Co. the start & drove the Indians in the hills on our side. Only a few of them stood their ground, & that to their sorrow. H Co. made for & surrounded the herd of about 300 ponies, while we dismounted & clambered up the hill after the Indians. The hills were from 70 to 100 feet high & very steep. We were obliged to clamber on our hands and knees & grab on bushes for assistance to reach the top. All this time the Indians were shooting at the Co. in their camp, who were so far away that they did but little harm, and paying little or no attention to us, once in a while a bullet would whistle pretty close. As soon as our heads popped over the hill (which was nearly all at the same time) they took fright & ran for the ravines, with few exceptions who stood their ground behind trees or rocks. There was some trees & lots of undergrowth on these hills. Here our 2nd Lieut. Fuller[32] was wounded, in the right shoulder. By this time our horses was brought up & we had lots of fun, driving them from one ravine to another for

---

32. Alfred M. Fuller (1852–1902), of Pennsylvania, graduated from West Point in 1876. He joined the Second Cavalry later that year, ultimately being stationed at Fort Ellis, Montana Territory. With Company F in the attack on Lame Deer's village on May 7, 1877, Fuller was wounded in the right shoulder. Carried on the disabled list from June 10, 1877, to September 23, 1878, he thereafter returned to frontier duty, serving at Forts Ellis and Custer in Montana, and Fort Snelling in Minnesota. Later he served at Fort Walla Walla and Vancouver Barracks, Washington Territory, and Fort Leavenworth, Kansas. In 1890, Fuller won a brevet of captain for his performance in the Lame Deer Fight. Later that year he saw duty in the Sioux Campaign at Pine Ridge, South Dakota. Promoted captain in the Second Cavalry in 1893, Fuller worked at the Rebellion Record Office until shortly before the outbreak of the Spanish-American War, when he accompanied his regiment to Cuba. He remained there until 1902, when he took leave to Chicago, where he died at age fifty. George W. Cullum, *Biographical Register of the Officers and Graduates of the U.S. Military Academy at West Point, N.Y., from its Establishment, in 1802, to 1890* (Boston: Houghton Mifflin and Company, 1891, and since supplemented at ten-year intervals to the present), 3:270; 4:274; 5:251.

about 5 miles. Quite a party of Indians that we were chas-
ing went down on the creek 2 miles below & attacked our
ammunition packs. They killed one man of our co. &
wounded one of L & captured 2 packs. The rest of the men
& packs went back to the infantry who were on their way
with the remainder of our pack outfit. The news of the
fight hurried them up some, & by 4 P.M. they got in the
Indian camp, where we had been ever since 10 A.M., the
fight being all over by this time excepting with the pickets.
Odd Indians would skulk up & send a shot at them. Our
co. had 2 killed & 3 wounded. H Co., 1 killed & 2 wounded.
G & L, no killed but several wounded. One of our men,
who was killed with the pack, & when found had no head.
They had beat it all to jelly between two rocks. I don't
know the exact number of Indians killed, but I think between 17 & 20. There were many.[33] It has been reported by
one of their party at the Red Cloud Agency[34] that 40 of

---

33. Casualties among Zimmer's unit, Company F, Second Cavalry,
consisted of two men killed—Privates Frank Glackowsky and Charles
A. Martindale; and two wounded—Private Samuel Freyer and Trum-
peter William C. Osmer. Including these, total army casualties at the
Lame Deer Fight numbered four men killed and four wounded. Indian
casualties totaled about fourteen dead, including several women. See
Greene, *Yellowstone Command*, 211, 212-13, 293. Lakota mutilations of
their dead enemies were motivated by retaliatory rage and were intended to remain with their victims in the afterlife. Anthony McGinnis,
*Counting Coup and Cutting Horses: Intertribal Warfare on the Northern Plains,
1738–1889* (Evergreen, Colo.: Cordillera Press, Inc., 1990), 28-29. A contemporary explanation for the practice of mutilation is in Richard Irv-
ing Dodge, *Our Wild Indians: Thirty-three Years' Personal Experience among
the Red Men of the Great West* (Hartford, Conn.: A. D. Worthington and
Company, 1883), 180-81.

34. Red Cloud Agency, located in extreme northwestern Nebraska
below Dakota Territory and the Great Sioux Reservation, was agency
home for the Oglala Sioux.

their wounded died during the following night for the want of shelter & surgical aid.[35]

At the time of the charge Chief Lame Deer ran out towards Miles, shaking a white rag, shook hands with the general, & on Miles's giving orders to have his gun taken away, he stepped back, aimed at Miles & killed an H Co. man nearly in rear of Miles. The chief & all the rest that remained in camp were sent to the Happy Hunting grounds by the first train. There was but 4 squaws in the whole party, 2 of which were killed.[36] This tribe was the Minneconjou Indians, a supply party for Sitting Bull.[37] (Only

---

35. This notation obviously reflected knowledge acquired at a later date, evidence that at least part of the journal's content was augmented by information derived later.

36. The incident that Zimmer described involved Miles's attempt to communicate with Lame Deer through an interpreter. The chief, who was dismounted, was armed with a Spencer carbine, and Miles, astride his horse, directed him to place the weapon on the ground. Lame Deer complied, but cocked the arm as he set it down, its muzzle pointed at Miles. When a scout indiscreetly aimed his gun at the chief, a commotion broke out. Lame Deer quickly grabbed his weapon, leveled it at Miles, and pulled the trigger. Immediately, the colonel swerved his mount. The bullet missed him, but struck and instantaneously killed his orderly, Private Charles Shrenger, Company H, Second Cavalry. Greene, *Yellowstone Command*, 208-10. In the ensuing battle, Lame Deer was killed, as were thirteen of his followers. Most of the members of Lame Deer's camp, including Lame Deer's son, Fast Bull, escaped into the hills.

37. Hardly "a supply party for Sitting Bull," the Minneconjous ("Those Who Plant By the Water") were one of the bands that composed the Teton Sioux, or Lakota, tribe. Sitting Bull (ca. 1834–1890), the acknowledged leader of the native coalition in 1876–77, had long resisted the inroads of white settlement in the area of the upper Missouri and Yellowstone drainages. Spurning the treaties of the 1860s to continue living in the old ways and places, the Hunkpapa medicine leader spearheaded opposition to the federal government's attempt to remove the tribesmen to the reservation and was at the core of the

for this party having all their ponies taken away & all of their
camping outfit burnt, which we did before leaving, & them
going to the Standing Rock Agency,[38] Sitting Bull would have
been on the warpath this summer.) Some of the boys said they
had arrows shot at them. There was any quantity of them in
their camp, also good Henry & Smith & Wesson rifles & lots
of stuff belonging to the 7th Cavalry that they got at the

---

assemblage that defeated Custer on the Little Bighorn. Only after Sitting Bull withdrew into Canada in 1877 and other Sioux surrendered
at the Dakota and Nebraska agencies did the army's campaign against
them conclude. Sitting Bull surrendered in 1881 at Fort Buford and eventually settled near the Cheyenne River Agency. As the Ghost Dance
movement peaked among the Sioux in 1890, he was killed by Indian
policemen during an attempted arrest. For the definitive biographical
treatment, see Robert M. Utley, *The Lance and the Shield: The Life and
Times of Sitting Bull* (New York: Henry Holt and Company, 1993). On
the Minneconjous, including reference to Lame Deer's genealogy, see
Kingsley M. Bray, "Lone Horn's Peace: A New View of Sioux-Crow
Relations, 1851–1858," *Nebraska History*, 66 (Spring 1985), 28–47. For
cultural and historical studies of the Lakotas, including the Minneconjous,
see George E. Hyde, *Red Cloud's Folk: A History of the Oglala Sioux Indians* (Norman: University of Oklahoma Press, 1937); George E. Hyde,
Spotted Tail's Folk: A History of the Brule Sioux (Norman: University of
Oklahoma Press, 1961); James C. Olson, *Red Cloud and the Sioux Problem*
(Lincoln: University of Nebraska Press, 1965); R. Eli Paul, ed., *Autobiography of Red Cloud: War Leader of the Oglalas* (Helena: Montana Histori-
cal Society Press, 1997); Robert W. Larson, *Red Cloud: Warrior Statesman
of the Lakota Sioux* (Norman: University of Oklahoma Press, 1997);
George E. Hyde, *A Sioux Chronicle* (Norman: University of Oklahoma
Press, 1956); Royal B. Hassrick, *The Sioux: Life and Customs of a Warrior
Society* (Norman: University of Oklahoma Press, 1964); and Raymond
J. DeMallie and Douglas R. Parks, eds., *Sioux Indian Religion: Tradition
and Innovation* (Norman: University of Oklahoma Press, 1987).

38. This reference to a later event—"going to Standing Rock
Agency"—reinforces the assumption that Zimmer likely transcribed his
journal from another journal or diary carried with him in 1877. Most of
the Lame Deer refugees eventually surrendered at Camp Sheridan, Nebraska, not at Standing Rock. Greene, *Yellowstone Command*, 22.

Custer massacre. The weather has been very fine all day, but at dark it comes to rain. Nearly every one is on the skirmish line. Indians are skulking about. They want their ponies.[39]

May 8th.

It was a dreadful rainy & cold night, but the day has been quite fair. This morning before leaving their camp we destroyed 53 lodges mostly of skins, any quantity of robes & several tons of jerked buffalo meat—in fact, everything. We built a fire at each tepee & put all its contents on. It was 10 A.M. before we left their camp. Miles had all his boys mounted on Indian ponies & saddles. Their saddles are little better than a sawbuck for either horse or rider. After we started, the drivers of the ponies had great trouble in keeping them together, so Gen. Miles had about 20 of the unruly ones shot. The Indians would fire a shot at our column as we moved along, but no one was hurt. We kept as far as possible from high bluffs. We moved down about 6 miles from the mouth of Muddy Creek on which the fight was, making 10 miles in all & went in camp on a large flat piece of ground clear of bluffs.

" *9th.*

Weather fine. We went down the river [Rosebud Creek] about 12 miles & met the trains & infantry. They had orders

---

39. The Lame Deer Fight constituted the last major action in the Great Sioux War. Following it, the refugees from Lame Deer's village gradually trickled into the agencies in Dakota and Nebraska. Through the remainder of the summer of 1877, troops canvassed the country below the Yellowstone in the vicinity of the Little Bighorn, Rosebud, Tongue, Powder, and Little Missouri rivers, as described by Zimmer below. For a comprehensive account of the Lame Deer campaign and its aftermath, see Greene, *Yellowstone Command,* 201-24.

to leave Tongue River & come across when we left & take their time. The whole outfit is camped together tonight.

May 10th.

It rained some last night & the day was nice until 4 P.M., when a heavy thunderstorm come on that will likely last all night. We laid in camp all day & the doctor is caring for the wounded. One of our men broke his arm and another put his shoulder out of place & one of H Co. broke his wrist & several others got hurt in various places, all in the charge by being thrown. And yet Gen. Miles says this was the best rough ground riding he ever saw.

" *11th.*

It rained some last night, but the morning opened up fine & remained so during the day. Moved down the river about 5 miles to get better grazing. Gen. Miles left us today, starting for Tongue River with 2 co. of infantry [and] L Co. of our battalion, taking the wounded in the ox train & all the loose ponies were herded along.

" *12th.*

Weather remains fair, grazing very good. The grass is from 5 to 6 inches high, the water in the Rosebud is rather bad. It tastes of alkali.

" *13th.*

Weather fair. L Co. was sent back today. Miles thought his infantry would be able to stand the Indians off should they be attacked. We changed camp again a few miles down. Our beef herd was stampeded last night by wolves (there being 23 head) & 18 of us went in search of them. Saw nothing of the beef, but brought in 2 mules & 5 ponies. This evening the balance of our co. went in search again.[40]

May 14th.

Weather very warm. This afternoon a little rain fell. The balance of our co. returned, but no cattle. They saw a few skulking Indians & it's supposed they have run them out of reach. A scout & 5 men started after dark for Tongue River Post to bring us more cattle. [In] the meanwhile we will have to live on jerked buffalo, some of which was brought from the Indian camp, for we have but little pork. (The Indians, besides drying the buffalo meat, they break the marrow bones & boil them. The marrow, it's put up in bladders & large intestines so that it will keep, & it's handy to carry about & keeps clean. They also dry the tripe of the buffalo. What kind of a dish they make out of it I never learned. In this Indian camp we just destroyed they had all kinds of cooking utensils, even crockery & china dishes. But everything was fearful dirty. They never wash their cooking utensils or dishes. After they have done using them they are chucked in a heap until wanted. They live principally on meat in their wild state. Some seasons of the year they get some roots which they eat for a change. We found a few in some of their tepees & they looked like artichokes.)[41]

---

40. The balance of the Second Cavalry battalion, under Captain Ball, remained in the field over the next several weeks attempting to run down the refugees from Lame Deer's village. As described below, the troops gradually scouted eastward from the Rosebud, eventually reaching the area of the Little Missouri River. Brisbin to AAGDD, October 26, 1877, in *Report of the Secretary of War, 1877,* 552.

41. These were most likely prairie turnips (also known as Indian breadroot) or wild carrots (yampa root), either of which was sometimes eaten raw but more often cooked and then sun-dried for future consumption. Jeff Hart, *Montana Native Plants and Early Peoples* (Helena: Montana Historical Society Press, 1976), 61-65.

" *15th.*

Weather cold. Had a heavy rain fall last night. Moved up the Rosebud 2 miles above Muddy Creek. Saw a few Indians on the bluffs on our way. Grazing not as good as below.

May 16th.

Weather pleasant. Some time during the night a message & some mail was sent to Tongue River Post by 4 men. It's reported that we are to scout the tributaries of the Rosebud. Shortly after we started, one of L Co. men found a nice Smith & Wesson rifle. It's supposed that an Indian was crawling around last night & forgot where he left it in the darkness, or one of the skiddadlers might have threw it away during the fight. It's only 3 miles across the hills to the battleground. We made a very late camp & wood is scarce. The water is a little better than below.

" *17th.*

Weather fair. We made but a few miles when we came to a halt, took 3 days rations on our horses, left the infantry & teams, & started up the river. We went but a few miles when we came to a branch of the Rosebud & took up it, the country being beautiful, very rolling and full of little valleys, with rivulets running down to the larger one. These streams are lined with flowers & flowering shrubs, also strawberries & others. We saw quite a number of buffalo & by 4 P.M. we got one for supper. After supper was over, it being about 6 P.M., we started off again & shortly after [it] commenced to rain. About 8 it rained so hard & became so dark that we went in camp in a steep ravine. By this time, we had got quite up in the world in a range of mountains called Wolf Mountains.

May 18th.

We spent a miserable night, it raining all the time, and at daylight, still raining, we saddled up and were soon on our way where God only knows. On [and] on we went & the rain fell faster. About 10 A.M. we got lost & went circling around & came back to our own trail, we being up in the clouds, we were unable to see even a distant mountain for a landmark. (We should be near the Little Horn River.) We found a ravine with water & lots of wood. Here we unsaddled our horses & commenced to kindle fires, which was an awful job, everything being soaking wet, as well as we. After fires were going, breakfast was soon prepared & ate, which made everyone feel much better. Here we waited for it to clear off, but night came & it [is] still raining.

" 19th.

It still rains & rained all night, besides the weather up here has been very cold. We spent a miserable night setting in the rain in our wet clothes & wrapped in our wet blankets, turning first one side then the other to the fire until daylight. Our horses haven't ate scarcely any. They stand in groups shivering with the cold, all humped up. A pitiful sight. After breakfast we saddled & were soon on our way back to the wagon train. We soon came to 4 inches of snow & here the rain had stopped. Now we could see the valley of the Little Horn, and in the distance the constant snow-covered Big Horn Mountains. This lasted but a short time, for our descent soon brought us in a rainy region again. We traveled pretty fast, as we wanted to make the train before dark. Some of the horses began to show signs of weakness, & as the air was a little milder here, we let the horses graze for an hour (while the men toiled about to get warm, for there was no wood here to make fires). Then off we went, but soon one of G Co. horses laid down & all the persuasion they could give him couldn't induce him to get up, so they went on and left him. This soon became a constant occurrence & before we reached the train in the evening some 30 were left out of the different companies. Our co. left 5, some of the best looking horses in the whole Co.[42] (It was supposed that if any got strength enough within a few days, they would take the trail and catch up, but none ever did. With[out] doubt the wolves polished lots of their bones while they lay in a helpless condition.) After we reached the train (it still raining) we put up our tents, which were in the wagons, ate supper & turned in in our wet clothing & blankets.

May 20th.
It rained all night. Also raining this morning & continued to until 9 A.M. Then the sun came out almost unbearable. This soon dried our clothes & blankets & at 4 P.M. we started down the river where there was more grass & wood. We had to go but a few miles to find both.

May 21st.
Weather pleasant. We left camp early & moved down 2 miles below Muddy Creek. H Co. & some of our officers went up to the battleground. The Indians had been back &

---

42. Zimmer's figure of five horses abandoned by Company F conforms with that given in Regimental Returns of the Second Cavalry, Return for May 1877. However, his figures for horses abandoned by the other companies are much higher than those officially reported. National Archives Microfilm Publication M744, Roll 166 (hereafter NAMP M744, Roll 16).

skinned the ponies & carried off some of the flesh. Only one of our dead had been disturbed, & that by wolves.

" *22nd.*
Weather quite chilly, rained again last night. We moved down to where we met the trains two days after the fight.

" *23rd.*
Weather squally. Pulled up pins. As usual, our march is down. This evening we are camped where 200 miners had themselves fortified against Indians in '72 [1874] for 2 days. They were unable to ascend the Rosebud & were obliged to retreat to the Yellowstone skirmishing most of the way. There was some killed on both sides, I couldn't learn how many.[43] Shortly after we got in camp, a party of our boys that went to Tongue River Post from time to time returned, bringing 20 head of beef & some mail.

" *24th.*
Weather fair until this evening. Laid over. This evening we are having a terrific thunderstorm. The thunder crashes the loudest & the lightning is the most vivid I ever saw.

---

43. Zimmer referred to the Yellowstone Wagon Road and Exploring Expedition, privately organized in Bozeman late in 1873 and underway early the following year. Its purpose was to find a route between Bozeman and the head of navigation on the Yellowstone, as well as to determine gold-mining potential in the region. The expedition numbered some 147 men and included more than two hundred horses and mules, besides twenty-two wagons drawn by oxen. It experienced several run-ins with Lakotas, one of which, in late March, occurred in the area of lower Rosebud Creek, and is the incident to which Zimmer alluded. In fact, only one citizen was wounded in the attack, and the expedition—far from retreating down the Yellowstone—pushed forward in its return to Bozeman, which it reached in May. Topping, *Chronicles of the Yellowstone*, 104-22; Brown, *Plainsmen of the Yellowstone*, 211-19.

" *25th.*

Weather quite warm until this evening, when we had a hail-storm, which turned to rain. One of G Co. men shot himself in the left shoulder last night while on guard, purely accidently.

May 26th.

Weather has been hot all day. We left our old camp & started across the divide to Tongue River. Here we went down as far as where we camped on the 5th, or where Miles had his fight last winter.[44] There's graves of 3 of his men here. Perhaps it was the thoughts of the fight last winter that made 2 of our men hostile enough to have one. After they got through, W. had to wear one of his eyes in a sling & looks as though his hostile stepmother had blown at his face. Tongue River is very high & awful muddy.

" *27th.*

Weather very warm. It's reported that the mail brought orders for us to return to the Yellowstone. The river is so high that we can't cross, so we have to move down this northeast side. We had to take to the hills most of the time (as there's less valley on this side than the other) & the teams had to have a great deal of help.

" *28th.*

Weather warm & another rough day's work for the teams. Only for them being nearly light it would [be] impossible for to take this route. We passed through some small flats where the grass was knee high to the horses. This grass is called Blue Joint. It's much like the Kentucky Blue Grass, only wider

---

44. This was the Wolf Mountains battle of January 8, 1877.

blades. (Our horses are living high. 3 quarts of corn & lots of this good grass makes them show flesh.)

" *29th.*
Weather quite cool. Our route was some better. Y & T, both of our co., had a few rounds of the manly art [boxing], as it is called. T soon squealed & wanted to go home. This evening we are having another rain, hail, thunder & lightning storm.

May 30th.
Weather cold & it rained all day & the road was the worst of any that we had on the whole trip. Tonight we are camped with an ox train which got stuck. They were coming to meet us with supplies.

" *31st.*
Weather cold. It rained all last night & today, sometimes snowing. The river is ¾ of a mile wide, instead of 3 rods, as it is at low water, & the water is thick with mud. We remained in camp all day & drew oats for our horses. They get 12 quarts when they get their full allowance.

June 1st.
It rained all last night & nearly all day. The sun came out, at times quite warm. The river is lowering fast. Went to the bank of the river to see a co. of infantry drill mounted on Indian ponies who are on the opposite side. The sight was very amusing. Some of the ponies never had anyone on them. This afternoon we moved to within 16 miles of Tongue River Post.

" *2nd.*
Weather pleasant. We moved to within 4 miles of the post this

forenoon. Rattlesnakes are very plenty. One was killed today with 12 rattles on.

" 3d.
The latter part of the day has been fine. Had some rain this
morning. Moved down to the post this afternoon. Four
steamboats have been up here since we left, with supplies.

" 4th.
More rain this morning. Grazing is poor here, but the horses
get more grain to make up.

June 5th.
Very pleasant this forenoon. For a change we had a wind &
rainstorm.

" 6th.
Weather fair. Moved up the Yellowstone River 5 miles.
Grazing very good.

" 7th.
Weather cool. Steam boats are arriving at the post daily.
Three are reported as lying there at present.

" 8th.
Weather fair. Six of our beef cattle swam the Yellowstone
& got away. We had mounted target practice this afternoon.
This is to be continued.[45]

---

45. Target practice, previously sporadic and governed by niggardly
ammunition allotments, increased for the army following the Little
Bighorn disaster in 1876. Douglas C. McChristian, *An Army of Marksmen: The Development of United States Army Marksmanship in the 19th
Century* (Fort Collins, Colo.: The Old Army Press, 1981), 33-34.

" *9th.*

Weather fine. 3 cos. of the first infantry came & camped near us today. The 3 cos. of the 22nd who were with us are on their way to Fort Wayne, Michigan.[46]

" *10th.*

It rained last night, & it's been quite cold all day. Cos. L & G were scouting amongst the hills & returned this evening with 12 ponies & mules. A steam boat passed our camp this evening enroute for the Big Horn Post with 3 cos. of the 11th Infantry on board.[47]

" *11th.*

Some rain today. Everything quiet on the Yellowstone.

" *12th.*

Rained all night & some during the day. Cold again.

------

46. Companies B, G, H, and K, First Infantry, commanded by Major Henry M. Lazelle, reached the Tongue River Cantonment on May 23, 1877, as reinforcement to Miles's force. Six companies of the Twenty-second Infantry had been in Montana since the previous August, having joined the troops prosecuting the Sioux and Northern Cheyennes at the same time as Miles and his Fifth Infantry soldiers. Greene, *Yellowstone Command*, 32, 215.

47. The soldiers of the Eleventh Infantry, assigned from the Cheyenne River and Standing Rock agencies in Dakota, were en route to assist in the construction of the Big Horn Post, soon to be renamed Fort Custer, at the junction of the Little Bighorn and Bighorn rivers, near where present Hardin, Montana, stands today. That post, along with the Tongue River Cantonment, was strategically located to monitor the situation with the Sioux and Northern Cheyennes during the months following the Little Bighorn disaster. Ibid., 185. For the history of Fort Custer, see Richard Upton, comp., ed., *Fort Custer on the Big Horn, 1877–1898* (Glendale, Calif.: The Arthur H. Clark Co., 1973). It was from Fort Custer that Zimmer received his discharge from the army in 1881.

" *13th*.

Weather quite cold. Our boys played the 5th Infantry boys another game of base ball & we're ahead again. Hurrah.

" *14th*.

A horrible thunder storm last night & a little rain fell during the day. Moved downstream a little way for better grass.

" *15th*.

Weather generally fair. A little rain this evening. Splendid cat fishing here. The boys catch lots, & large ones.

" *16th*.

Weather very warm. Just right for lying in the shade & dream of the good times that's coming, boys. A detail of 20 men went out of our battalion to drive a herd of beef cattle over to Powder River 40 miles for the 7th Cavalry & some of the 22nd Infantry, who are to scout that region.[48] I went in the Yellowstone a-bathing for the first time. The water is very cold yet & the current is so swift one is obliged to swim if he goes in 3 ft of water, & swimming is very easy, but the landing is not. It's impossible to swim upstream.

---

48. Miles directed Major Henry M. Lazelle to scout for the remnants of Lame Deer's band in the direction of the Little Missouri River, and also to weigh the potential of establishing a wagon road between the cantonment and the Black Hills. Lazelle's command consisted of two companies of his First Infantry, the battalion of the Twenty-second that was en route east, one company of the Seventh Cavalry, a party of scouts, and an artillery piece, besides the beef herd noted by Private Zimmer. Lazelle to AAGDD, September 5, 1877 ("Reconnaissance in Country East of Powder River, by Maj. H. M. Lazelle, First Infantry"), in *Report of the Secretary of War, 1877*, 574. Lazelle's command later interacted with those of Captain Ball and Major Brisbin as they maneuvered in the region of the Montana-Dakota border tracking the remnants of Lame Deer's Sioux.

June 17th.

Weather warm & windy. About 7 P.M. a party of 20 Indians attacked a herding party of 15. Several rounds were fired on both sides. One herder was wounded badly. If any Indians were wounded, it [is] not known. No one was killed on either side. The Indians got no horses or cattle, but they [the herders] lost 2 ponies. This occurred across the river & as soon as help was starting across on the ferry they skipped (the Indians).⁴⁹

" 18th.

Weather as yesterday. During the afternoon the detachment returned that went to Powder River. This morning they saw a few Indians. They gave them chase & got 13 of their loose ponies. It is supposed that they were some of the same party that tackled our herders. (Indians always drive from 2 to 4 loose ponies apiece along when they go any great distance & the saddle is changed from 2 to 4 times a day.)

---

49. An official account of this action stated: "Just after retreat a party of possibly 30 or 35 mounted Indians made a dash on a little camp, consisting of Corporal Miller and 14 privates of the Second Cavalry, who were engaged in guarding a small quantity of government transportation on the north side of the Yellowstone, which, owing to the ferry being out of order, it had been impossible to cross. The affair lasted probably some 20 minutes, the enemy being most handsomely repulsed, the only animals captured being two citizen's ponies, which the Bozeman mail party had failed to picket. Casualties, infantry soldier slightly wounded in the calf of the leg. Companies A and K, Fifth Infantry, crossed over temporarily to the relief of Corporal Miller's party." Major George Gibson to AAGDD, October 1, 1877 (Report on Cantonment at Tongue River, Montana), in *Report of the Secretary of War, 1877,* 543-44. However, Captain Simon Snyder noted in his diary that the relief force never crossed the stream. "Diary of Simon Snyder, Captain, Co. F, 5th U.S. Infantry" (manuscript in the library of Little Bighorn Battlefield National Monument, Crow Agency, Montana).

MONTANA TERRITORY

Glendive Cantonment

Tongue River Cantonment

Fort Abraham Lincoln

Bismarck

Yellowstone River

Bighorn River

Powder River

Tongue River

Little Missouri R.

Cannonball

Cedar

Grand River

Missouri River

BIG HORN MOUNTAINS

Crazy Woman

Clear Fork

Little Powder

Short Pine Hills

Slim Buttes

Deadwood

Black Hills

Cantonment Reno

WYOMING TERRITORY

DAKOTA TERRITORY

Area of the Little Missouri Expedition
July 28 – September 1, 1877

⟨∘∘∘⟨∘∘∘⟨∘∘∘ Route of Major Brisbin's Command

Camp Robinson

Red Cloud Agency

NEBRASKA

Approximately 100 miles

MAP BY JEROME A. GREENE AND KATHRYN FEHLIG

" *19th*.

Rained last night & some during the day. The Yellowstone is booming (lots of rain must have fell up above some days ago).

" *20th*.

Rained again last night. It also rained some today. On the night of the 17th two horse thieves ran off 25 head of horses & ponies from Tongue River Post. This afternoon a party of mounted infantry brought them and their plunder back. They were making for the Black Hills. This evening an-

other boat passed up for the Big Horn Post loaded with
building material & 2 cos. of the 11th Infantry.

June 21st.
Weather very warm. Target practice is discontinued.

" *22nd.*
Rained some last night & yet it's very warm. Moved camp
for better grass downstream ½ mile.

" *23rd.*
It commenced raining this morning & never let up till noon.
The afternoon has been cool & pleasant. Everything is lovely.

" *24th.*
Weather cool & windy. White[50] of our co. who has been
with Lieut. Doane, returned to the co. for his discharge, his
time being out. Says Doane has 800 [Crow] warriors under
him & that they have been up & across the headwaters of
Big Horn River, Little Horn, Rosebud, Powder & return
again to the mouth of the Big Horn. He says that buffalo
are plenty on the Big Horn & that the Indians killed 1500
one afternoon. (About all they take is the robes & some
choice bits where they are so plenty. The buffalo are traveling north across the Yellowstone.) On their scout they saw
no Sioux or any signs of there having been any lately. They
are going over to the Musselshell River where the buffalo

---

50.   This was Private William H. White, whose reminiscence of
his army service, written ca. 1930–32, appears in *Custer, Cavalry & Crows:
The Story of William White as Told to Thomas Marquis*, annotated by John
A. Popovich (Fort Collins, Colo.: The Old Army Press, 1975). The circumstances of White's discharge are noted on 122-23.

are going, thinking they may find some of the Sioux over there hunting.[51] White is going back to the Crows & buy a young squaw. He says that he can get a nice one & a good worker, 16 years old, by giving the old folks about $40 worth of presents. He is going to stay awhile with this tribe as a trader. He can speak the Crow language quite well for the time he has been there, so he says, & by getting the squaw will soon get it thorough.[52] There is but a few words in any of the Indian languages, one word has meaning for a dozen different things. For instance, (Hamnet) means "no I can't," "haven't got any," "won't do it," and various other words & sentences of this nature. They have no names for a brook, creek, river, lake or pond. It's either a large water or a small water with them. They also have a kind of a dumb language, which they all know. They don't have any alphabet, like our dumb, and spell every word, but on the contrary, one nod of the head, a flick of the arm, or a sudden twist of the wrist means more than one could put on this sheet. They couldn't find one-fifth words enough in their language to describe a dress of a girl of the period.[53]

---

51. Lieutenant Doane's movement with the Crows is described in ibid., 118- 22.

52. White subsequently found and married a Crow girl, Yoho-na-ho, remaining with her until her death in 1921. White later served as a guide at Custer Battlefield National Monument. He died in 1938. Ibid., 130-31, 180, 182.

53. Zimmer's comments about Indian languages, and the Crow language in particular, are vastly oversimplified; however, his remarks about the multiplicity of meanings for individual Crow words and expressions, as well as for body language, is substantiated in Lowie, *Crow Indians*, 104. The sign, or gesture, language enabled individuals from the Crow and other tribes to communicate with one another. An authoritative treatment appears in William P. Clark, *The Indian Sign Language* (Philadelphia: L. R. Hamersly and Company, 1885).

June 25th.

Weather very cool with occasional showers.

" *26th.*

Weather is warm, against that of yesterday. It was near being a frost last night. I Co. of the 7th Cavalry went up to Custer's battleground on the Little Horn River to bring away some of the officers' remains.[54] A co. of the 5th cavalry are camped near us this evening.

" *27th.*

Quite pleasant today after a heavy rain last night. 225 citizens came upon a boat, mechanics & laborers to build a post on the Little Horn River near the mouth of the Big Horn. 100 of the workmen are to remain here and build this post up. The other 125 will go up [to] the [Big] Horn.

" *28th.*

Weather remains pleasant. Rattlesnakes are getting so plenty that they are no more a curiosity but a nuisance. Every evening while we are going to catch up our horses from 1 to 4 are killed. They are from 18 to 30 inches long & have from 1 to 8 rattles.

---

54. Company I, Seventh Cavalry, accompanied Lieutenant Colonel Michael V. Sheridan, brother of General Philip H. Sheridan, to the Little Bighorn battlefield to retrieve the remains of Custer and other officers for reburial elsewhere, with Custer eventually being interred at West Point, New York. Michael Sheridan also supervised the reburial on the field of the remains of enlisted men killed there. An account by Sheridan appears in the *Chicago Times,* July 15, 1877, but see also *Army and Navy Journal,* July 28, 1877, and Richard G. Hardorff, *The Custer Battle Casualties: Burials, Exhumations, and Reinterments* (El Segundo, Calif.: Upton and Sons, Publishers, 1989), chap. 4.

June 29th.

The day opened & closed raining. 25 men were detailed from our battalion to escort a pack train that is going with A Co. 5th Cavalry to Ft. Reno[55] below Ft. Lincoln on the Missouri River. Our boys are to be gone but a few days & bring back the mules who are carrying oats when they are used up.

" 30th.

Weather fair. An order has been received to discharge all enlisted men having but 4 months to serve, so as to reduce the Army from 30,000 to 25,000. 8 men were discharged out of our co.[56]

July 1.

It's been a cold & rainy day. During last night & today 3 boats arrived loaded with lumber.

" 2nd.

Weather fair. 75 lodges of Indians belonging to different tribes that were camped about the post have been moved

---

55. Zimmer is in error regarding Fort Reno. He means Cantonment Reno, established October 12, 1876, on the Powder River in Wyoming Territory as a supply base for Brigadier General George Crook's operations against the Sioux and Northern Cheyennes. Frazer, *Forts of the West*, 183. In April 1877, the Fifth Cavalry, from Fort D. A. Russell, near Cheyenne, occupied the cantonment during scouting forays into the Bighorn–Powder River areas of Wyoming and Montana, and in June, Company A, under Captain Calbraith P. Rogers, was at Tongue River. *Cheyenne Daily Leader*, July 12, 1877.

56. An act of Congress of August 5, 1876, directed the reduction of the army to 25,000 men. To effect the law, General Order No. 47, May 9, 1877, mandated the suspension of recruiting, with minor exceptions, and "the discharge of all soldiers whose terms of enlistment would expire prior to October 31, 1877." *Report of the Secretary of War, 1877*, iii.

across Tongue River opposite the post. These Indians came in and gave themselves up, turned in their arms & ponies, & say they will never go on the warpath again. (Gen. Miles returned them one pony to the family for amusement I suppose.)[57] A & G Cos. of our battalion were ferried across the Yellowstone to the north side this evening. It's quite a curiosity to go to the Quartermaster storehouse & see the different kind of firearms the Indians turned in. Some of the first ever invented, muzzle-loading shotguns & rifles with flintlocks, others with caplock, some old rifles with barrels as large around as a chair leg & as long as a school boy going on an errand. Besides [these], they had some of the latest breechloaders for metallic shells.[58] These Indians at Tongue River

---

57. These Indians comprised 291 Northern Cheyennes and 19 Sioux who had surrendered at the Tongue River Cantonment in April 1877, following Miles's success at the Battle of Wolf Mountains in January and the prolonged period of negotiation with the Indians that followed that encounter. Most of the people with Crazy Horse and other leaders surrendered at Camp Robinson, Nebraska, a month later in May. Zimmer's estimate of the number of lodges is high, with forty-five tepees probably being more accurate. "Report of Indians that surrendered or were captured through the exertions of the troops in the District of the Yellowstone," Fort Keogh, M.T., December 15th 1881, box T-2, folder, Nelson A. Miles Papers, Fifth Infantry, Fort Keogh, M.T., U.S. Army Military History Institute, Army War College, Carlisle Barracks, Pennsylvania. For background on the Northern Cheyennes, some of whom served Miles as scouts during the closing operations of the Sioux War, see Peter Powell, *Sweet Medicine: The Continuing Role of the Sacred Arrows, the Sun Dance, and the Sacred Buffalo Hat in Northern Cheyenne History*, 2 vols. (Norman: University of Oklahoma Press, 1969); George Bird Grinnell, *The Cheyenne Indians*, 2 vols. (New Haven: Yale University Press, 1923); George Bird Grinnell, *The Fighting Cheyennes* (Norman: University of Oklahoma Press, 1956); and Greene, *Yellowstone Command*, 196-98.

58. The varieties of arms given up by the Indians at the time of their surrender at Tongue River are enumerated in Douglas Scott and Dick Harmon, "General Nelson Miles' List of Surrendered Sioux War Guns," *Man at Arms*, 15 (January/February 1993), 31-36.

get government rations, but only three days at a time, &
they are allowed no firearms of any kind. (Later, Nov. 17th.
It's reported that General Miles has shipped these Indians,
along with the Nez Perces, to the Indian Territory. I suppose you have already heard about Joseph's band, not those
of the children of Israel.[59])

July 3rd.
Weather warm. This morning H & G Cos. shipped on the
steamer *Arkansas Jo*[60] for Glendive Creek, about 200 [100]

---

59. This parenthetical reference to later events further suggests that
the body of the existing journal was transcribed by Zimmer some time
after the day-to-day activities were initially recorded, probably in a
diary that is now long lost. On Chief Joseph, see part 2, footnote 28,
below. Seventeen Northern Cheyennes accompanied the Nez Perce
prisoners south in the fall of 1877. The Cheyennes joined their surviving kinsmen, who had surrendered the previous spring, at the Darlington
Agency near Fort Reno, Indian Territory (present Oklahoma). Conditions at that place, together with a longing to be in their northern
homeland, led many of the Northern Cheyenne families to flee Fort
Reno in September 1878. Some of the people under Chief Little Wolf
surrendered at Fort Keogh, Montana, and were permitted to remain
there, presaging the origin of the Northern Cheyenne Reservation in
Montana Territory. Orlan J. Svingen, *The Northern Cheyenne Indian Reservation* (Niwot, Colo.: University Press of Colorado, 1993), 20-21. The
others under Chief Dull Knife were captured and imprisoned at Fort
Robinson, Nebraska. In January 1879, these people broke out of their
barracks-jail, and more than sixty died attempting to flee the soldiers.
The survivors were eventually allowed to return to Montana. Utley,
Frontier Regulars, 283-84; Powell, *Sweet Medicine*, 1:276.
    60. The *Arkansas*—not *Arkansas Jo*—was a wood-hulled sternwheel
packet measuring 185 feet by 36 feet built in Pennsylvania in 1868 for the
Arkansas River–New Orleans cotton trade. In 1871 the vessel began trans-
porting grain and goods in the upper Mississippi region. Sunk in 1876,
the *Arkansas* was raised and used on the Missouri and Yellowstone until
1884, when it sunk again. Frederick Way, Jr., comp., *Way's Packet Directory,
1848–1983* (Athens: Ohio University Press, 1983), 29.

miles down the river. The detachment that went with the
pack train returned at noon with 30 empty pack mules.

" *4th.*

Weather very warm all day. At 2 A.M. we were aroused to
pack up & ship on the steamer *J. M. Chambers*[61] of St. Louis
for Glendive Creek. After putting some rations & forage
on, besides our horses & 50 head of pack mules, we pulled
out by 7 A.M.[62] In a few minutes we reached Miles City 3
miles below. Here the boat held up and took in 5 cords of
wood. (This place was started last fall, with 3 log cabins
occupied by wood choppers working for the government.
Now there's 14 log structures besides quite a number of
tents. The places of business are 3. 2 drinking places & one

---

61. The *John M. Chambers*, completed at St. Louis in 1875, was a
sternwheel packet with wooden hull that measured 174 feet by 32 feet.
The craft burned in 1876, but was repaired and continued to ply the
upper Missouri waters. Beginning in the late seventies, the *John M.
Chambers* carried cotton on the lower Mississippi. In 1884 she hit a
snag and burned again. Ibid., 253.

62. On July 4, Companies F, G, and H, of the Second Cavalry
battalion, augmented by one company of the Seventh Cavalry, two
mounted companies of the Fifth Infantry, and a large body of Crow
scouts, all under the command of Captain Ball, and later of Major
Brisbin, departed the cantonment on a scout that led them into
Dakota Territory over a course of nearly 600 miles and returned them
to the mouth of Tongue River on August 30. The movement, one of
several programmed by Miles to scour the region for the refugees of
Lame Deer's village, as well as to examine potential wagon routes, partly
coincided with that headed by Major Lazelle that ranged southeast to
the Little Missouri and into Dakota, and another directly under Miles
that inspected the country between the Yellowstone and Missouri
rivers. Greene, *Yellowstone Command*, 221-22; Regimental Returns of
the Second Cavalry, Return for July, 1877, NAMP M744, Roll 166;
Major George Gibson to AAGDD, October 1, 1877, in *Report of the
Secretary of War, 1877*, 546.

store.)[63] This took but a few minutes, then it drifted on. The country is much the same as the upper part of the Yellowstone, only there is less timber & islands. In some places the banks for miles at a time are a solid mass of coal. Sometimes there [is] not a foot of earth on it and how far it goes below the water no one knows. At one place in the bend of the river where the water had cut under, huge pieces had broken off & rolled down the size of a [railroad] car. A little below Powder River we saw the wreck of the steamer *Osceola,*[64] which was wrecked on the 15th of June in a heavy wind storm. It cleared her decks of cabin, engine & boilers, & the crew barely escaped with their lives. As it was, some got injured & the cabin furniture could still be seen scattered along the bank, the piano laid up high & dry. Our ride was very pleasant until 25 miles below, when our boat ran on a sand bar. The crew worked till after dark

---

63. Miles City—originally Milestown or Milesburg—named for Nelson A. Miles, evolved in the area east of the Tongue River Cantonment over the course of the year following the post's establishment. Miles's nephew, George Miles, of Westminster, Massachusetts, was one of the first entrepreneurs, cultivating a sheep-raising industry and eventually other businesses in support of the military presence. George Miles held one of the earliest land claims in the region. He profited from sales of this property and from his involvement in numerous enterprises, among them hardware, lumber, and banking. He remained a fixture in Miles City until his death in 1935. *Miles City Daily Star,* January 16, 1935; *Centennial Roundup* (Miles City, Mont.: Miles City Star, 1987), 43, 45; Warren Woodson, *Pioneering Tales of Montana* (New York: Exposition Press, 1965), 149-51.

64. The *Osceola* was destroyed by a tornado on June 22. Built in Osceola, Wisconsin, in 1874, she measured 130 feet by 22 feet, and took part in the cotton trade on the lower Mississippi. The *Osceola* sank in February 1876, with 300 bales aboard, but cargo and passengers were saved and the vessel raised. *Way's Packet Directory,* 358-59.

in trying to spar[65] her off. The steamer *Gen. Meade*[66] passed us at noon with lumber for Post.

July 5th.

Another very warm day. All hands went to work early at the spars. At 9 A.M. the mules were dumped in the river to lighten her up & yet she wouldn't float. Soon after the horses & then the men, all on a portion of the sand bar the boat stuck on. All to no purpose. She wouldn't float & work was continued till 9 P.M. We put in the night on the bar.

" *6th.*

A little rain fell last night & the air is much cooler. By 9 A.M. she floats, and by 12 M we were off again (after being shipwrecked on a barren island for 45 hours). We were 6 hours in going from here to Glendive Creek. The country

----

65. Sparring was one method by which vessels grounded on sand-bars freed themselves. "The spars were long, heavy timbers resembling telegraph poles, and a set of them, two in number, were always carried on the sides of the boat near the bow ready for use. When she became lodged on a bar, the spars were raised and set in the river bottom, like posts, their tops inclined toward the bow. Above the line of the deck each was rigged with a tackle-block over which a manila cable was passed, one end being fastened to the gunwhale of the boat and the other end wound around the capstan. As the capstan was turned and the paddle-wheel revolved, the boat was thus lifted and pushed forward. Then the spars were re-set farther ahead and the process repeated until the boat was at last literally lifted over the bar." Joseph Mills Hanson, *The Conquest of the Missouri; Being the Story of the Life and Exploits of Captain Grant Marsh* (Chicago: A. C. McClurg and Co., 1916), 86–87.

66. The *General Meade*, a sternwheel wood-hulled packet, 192 feet by 30 feet, was built in Pittsburgh in 1875. It ran on compound engines. Operating on the Missouri River during its early use, the vessel later plied the lower Mississippi. In 1888, the *General Meade* became snagged and was lost with four thousand sacks of wheat. *Way's Packet Directory*, 182.

was much the same as that above. Quite a number of our men got too much benzoate & were useless in unloading our stuff.[67] Two of our uncommissioned officers were on the spree and got reduced to the ranks. We landed on the south bank where H & G Cos. were in camp for several days, their boat having had good luck.

July 7th.

We had a nice shower last night & the day has been nice & cool. Glendive Creek empties in the Yellowstone on the south side. It's only a small stream & at the head of navigation, in low water. Boats are passing up & down continually. The *Tidal Wave*[68] stopped this afternoon and put off some rations for us. On the opposite bank of the Yellowstone there is some log barracks[69] that the 22nd Infantry built last fall to guard property that was put off here for Tongue River Post while [until] it was taken overland during the winter. Mosquitos bother us more here than any place we have been this summer.

---

67. What Zimmer calls benzoate is an alkaline compound containing magnesium sulfate found in area creeks and which evidently prostrated some of the men with diarrhea and cramping.

68. The *Tidal Wave*, built in Pennsylvania in 1870, measured 160 feet by 36 feet. Originally, she ran between Red River and New Orleans on the Mississippi, but after 1872 plied the upper Missouri. *Way's Packet Directory*, 454–55.

69. The Glendive Cantonment, a supply depot erected at the head of the seasonal low-water navigation of the Yellowstone, stood on the north bank of the Yellowstone, nearly opposite to the mouth of Glendive Creek. The post contained several log-hut quarters, barracks, and storehouses, the whole surrounded by an earthwork embankment fronting on the river, and was of critical importance in relaying supplies to the major Tongue River Cantonment, approximately 140 miles west by road up the Yellowstone. Greene, *Yellowstone Command*, 72.

" *8th.*

Weather cool. We broke camp at 9 A.M. & took 8 days rations on pack mules, besides some oats. The country the fore part of the day was very hilly & full of steep ravines, which gave us lots of trouble to take our 12 lb. Rodman Gun[70] along, which was drawn by 8 horses. Some times horses were un-hitched and a whole co. would be pulling on a drag rope to get her up where the horses could get footing again. The after part of the day it was a rolling prairie covered with blue joint grass. Wood & water was very scarce all day. About sunset we found a little of both & went in camp. There is a vine[71] growing here in Dakota Territory (in which territory we are)[72] that keeps green all summer & winter. The smell & foliage are like that of the red cedar. How nice this would be in the East for verandas & arbors if it would live. Flowers continue to bloom in spite of the dry weather. Every few days another variety puts in its appearance. The flowers that are natives of the hilly regions haven't as a general thing such long stems as those on the prairie or table land.

---

70. This was a 12-pounder Napoleon gun, a widely used weapon during the Civil War that could deliver shot or shell at ranges up to 1,700 yards. Zimmer here confuses it with the Model 1861 three-inch Ordnance Rifle, commonly called a Rodman gun because of its re-semblance to the larger smoothbore cannon of that name widely used during the Civil War. Warren Ripley, *Artillery and Ammunition of the Civil War* (New York: Promontory Press, 1970), 26-27, 162-63. Both the Napoleon gun and the Ordnance rifle gun were prominently used by Miles during the campaigns of 1876–77.

71. This was likely creeping Juniper (*Juniperus horizontalis*), a pros-trate and somewhat vinelike, mat-forming shrub prevalent throughout much of the northern plains. Great Plains Flora Association, *Flora of the Great Plains* (Lawrence: University Press of Kansas, 1986), 72.

72. Although Zimmer's unit was headed east, on July 8 it was still in Montana Territory.

July 9th.

Weather very warm. Country a beautiful rolling prairie. We passed a great number of prairie dog villages. There would be one on every mound & he'd give on [us?] a saucy reception. They chat much like the fox squirrel. About 4 P.M. we came on Beaver Creek. Its banks are lined with rose & berry bushes & they all tangled together with the wild hop vine. Rattlesnakes are very plenty along the stream. The water is the best that we have had since we left the upper part of the Yellowstone in April. Wood is not very plenty. The big gun gave us little trouble today. Saw a few deer & antelope.

" *10th.*

The weather has been cloudy & cool. Last night the dew wet the ground as though it had been raining. We kept up Beaver Creek all day. The country if anything it's prettier than yesterday. This would be a good place for sheep or cattle raising. Good water & grass plenty. Beaver must be very plenty in the creek, for their dams are very numerous. They are built of logs & brush, besides stones with layers of sod & earth. (I am of the opinion that they plant willows on them so their roots many help to hold them together, for nearly every dam has them growing on.)

July 11th.

The weather is a little warmer than yesterday, the country much the same. This evening we are camped on a creek with little water. It's only to be found in holes & that's stagnant & smells very bad. Last night, in watering our horses, one of the beaver dams was badly broken. This morning it's in good order. They must have worked most of the night. I have seen some stumps on the Yellowstone where the beaver has gnawed off trees 18 inches through. They also know enough to gnaw on the watery side so that they won't have to drag or roll their logs so far.

" *12th.*

We had a little shower this morning which made it quite cool for the time, but this afternoon it was warmer than ever. Major Lazelle[73] of the 1st Infantry came to scout the

------

73. Major Henry M. Lazelle (1832–1917), First Infantry, by 1877 was a veteran of twenty-two years in the army. He was from Massachusetts and graduated from West Point in 1855. Assigned to the Southwest with the Eighth Infantry, Lazelle saw service against the Apaches, in which he was wounded, before the outbreak of the Civil War took him east. During that conflict he rose to become colonel of the Sixteenth New York Cavalry and countered Confederate guerilla operations in the South. Between 1863 and 1864 Lazelle commanded the Cavalry Brigade of the Twenty-second Corps. During the war he fought at Culpeper, Virginia, where he exhibited "gallant and meritorious services in action." After the war Lazelle, as captain, Eighth Infantry, served on the expedition accompanying the Northern Pacific Railroad survey in 1871. He was promoted major in 1874. Following the Great Sioux War, he commanded Fort Sully, Dakota, built Fort Meade, Dakota, and was commandant of cadets, U.S. Military Academy, from 1879 to 1882, when he became lieutenant colonel, Twenty-third Infantry. Lazelle became colonel, Eighteenth Infantry, in 1889, and retired five years later. *Records of Living Officers of the United States Army*, 339; Heitman, *Historical Register*, 1:620.

Lazelle's scouting mission in the summer of 1877 resulted in the distinction of his having commanded during the last action of the Great Sioux War. On July 4, his Northern Cheyenne scouts engaged about fifteen refugees from Lame Deer's village near the "big bend" of the Little Missouri River. Lazelle's maneuver soon after deteriorated into an exercise of getting his command across the badlands terrain to reach the Yellowstone, where he re-outfitted before again moving out to cooperate with Major Brisbin's column. Greene, *Yellowstone Command*, 221. Lazelle then returned to the Yellowstone and reached the Tongue River Cantonment on September 1. See Lazelle to AAGDD, September 5, 1877, in *Report of the Secretary of War, 1877*, 575.

Little Missouri River about the first of June with 6 co. of infantry & B Co. 7th Cavalry. About noon & within 4 miles of the river (Little Missouri, I mean), we came across B Co. They had left the infantry & wagon train on the upper part of Beaver Creek, took pack mules & came in search of us, they having been informed of our presence in these parts by a scout who was sent out some days ago. They brought two days rations for us from their train. Tonight we are all camped at a large basin of water, & the water is so bad that it nearly gags one to drink of it. Wood is plenty, that is, for our use. (When I say water or wood is plenty, I don't mean that the country is full of it. I mean there is enough for our immediate [needs?], for off of large streams there is but very [little] wood & that far between, except in some parts of the mountains wood is plenty enough.) The country has been very fine until we came near the river. Then we came to what is known here as the Bad Lands, which are nearly destitute of vegetation or water (if you find any water, its alkali). For miles on a stretch, & for roughness, it's nearly as bad as the lava beds of northern California where the Modocs were in '70 ['73],[74] & on the other side it's said to be worse than this. Major Lazelle's outfit saw an Indian trail, but it was too large for one co. to follow it, & as for infantry, they are of no use on a chase. Maj. Lazelle's scouts came to us this evening, 8 in number, & the report is that we are to take up the trail & follow it. One of the scouts says they killed an Indian on the trail day before yesterday. He was in the rear spying about.

---

74. Reference is to the Modoc Indian War of 1872–73, which had received extensive newspaper coverage. For a comprehensive study, see Erwin N. Thompson, *Modoc War: Its Military History and Topography* (Sacramento: Argus Books, 1971).

July 13th.

Weather warm. Early this morning the big gun & 15 men were sent back to the wagon train with orders to move slowly down Beaver Creek so that we can overtake it on our way back. We saw the dead Indian in the trail & two ponies. The Indian had his hair lifted. The trail ran through the worst of Bad Lands all day just a few miles from the river. We passed 3 of their camping [sites?] during the day. Wood & water bad & scarce.

July 14th.

Weather very warm. We kept on the trail until it crossed the Little Missouri River. (The river looks much like Tongue River in low water. It empties in the Missouri proper 50 miles below where the Yellowstone does.) This was about noon. Here we turned back direct north towards Beaver Creek. On doing so, we crossed some of the worst country I've ever been in. Some of the bluffs are as red as brick & quite as hard, as they have the appearance of huge piles of rolling mill clinkers. What little [water] there [is] found in the ravines are alkali of different substances. Some of the water leaves a white coating, like chalk, on everything it comes in contact with. Other water leaves a pink or deep red coating. We crossed one high ridge where there had been a forest of cottonwood. They have been blown down or rotted off, with the exception of a few short stubs that are now petrified into solid stone, large trunks 40 & 50 feet long & from 2 to 3½ feet through. We travel through this last-mentioned country until nearly dark, when we found a spring of passable water with some wood growing about it & good grass, so we went in camp. The cause of our turning back was on account of not having rations but for a few days longer.

July 15th.

The weather has been cold & windy. So much so that the men kept on their overcoats nearly all day. About 4 P.M. we met Major Lazelle's camp on Beaver Creek, 25 miles below where our command camped on the 9th. The country to-day has been a lovely prairie. We camped close to Lazelle's command for the night. Game is very scarce.

" *16th.*

We were near having a frost last night. It's not as cold as yesterday, though the wind blows very fresh. We started in a north west direction this morning which soon took us on the trail we came from the Yellowstone & Glendive. Lazelle's command & train took a southwest course towards the Powder River. We are taking the big gun back with us. This evening we are camped where we camped on the 8th.

" *17th.*

Weather warm. We reached the Yellowstone early this afternoon. Our camp is nearly where it was 9 days ago [July 8]. This trip has been a severe one on our horses' backs. So much up & down hill work, along with their sweating, has sored many of them. They are all in good condition, yet they got no grain after the first day out.

" *18th.*

The day has been very pleasant. About 8 A.M. the steamer *Fanchon*[75] came down the river bringing Major Brisbin, who

---

75. The *Fanchon*, built in Pennsylvania in 1875, was a sternwheel packet with wooden hull measuring 174 feet by 35 feet. Used on the Yellowstone in 1877, the *Fanchon* saw wide use between Pittsburgh, Cincinnati, and New Orleans, where she was destroyed in a boiler explosion accident in 1882. *Way's Packet Directory*, 160.

has got over his illness, & will now take command. Shortly after she landed, orders were given to break camp & get aboard to be taken across. We are now camped near the log barracks [Glendive Cantonment]. Grass is much better here than on the other side. L Co. of our battalion who remained at Tongue River when we started down the Yellowstone, has since started for the National Park with Gen. Sherman & some other big guns.[76] Before L Co. left they got 4 months pay & in a drunken brawl between J. Clarry & P. Galy,[77] the former shot & seriously wounded the latter in the bowels.

July 19th.

Weather warm & so is the Yellowstone water & we are improving our time in it while it lasts.

---

76. Company L performed escort duty for Commanding General William T. Sherman, who visited the Yellowstone country in the summer of 1877 to assess the Indian situation (on July 17 he decreed "the Sioux Indian problem, as a war question, as solved"), inspect the new forts (Keogh and Custer) being built in the region, and tour Yellowstone National Park. At Tongue River, Sherman reviewed Miles's troops and pinned Medals of Honor on thirty-one men to honor their performance in the Great Sioux War. The other "big guns" were Dakota Department Commander Brigadier General Alfred H. Terry, Department Quartermaster Major Benjamin C. Card, and their aides. For details, see *Reports of Inspection Made in the Summer of 1877 by Generals P. H. Sheridan and W. T. Sherman of Country North of the Union Pacific Railroad* (Washington, D.C.: Government Printing Office, 1878).

77. These individuals were probably Privates Patrick McGauley and John Clary, both of whom were shown to be "in arrest by civil authority" as of July 17. Clary had enlisted September 11, 1876, in Cleveland, Ohio, while McGauley had enlisted September 16, 1876, in Boston. Regimental Returns of the Second Cavalry, Returns for July and August, 1877, NAMP M744, Roll 166; Muster Roll, Company L, Second Cavalry, June 30, 1877–August 31, 1877. RG 94, RAMR, NA.

" *20th.*

Weather the same as yesterday. Amusements, also swimming & fishing. Wood is rather scarce close to camp, so some of the men were sent up a small stream to cut some & this afternoon the pack train brought it in. This is one of the most efficient pack trains I ever saw. The common saying is, "as dumb as a mule," but I see by kind treatment that mules will learn quite as readily as horses. In the evening when we make camp, the mules are unsaddled in a line (each saddle is numbered with a large white figure on top) & the saddles put in a line in front of the mules. In the morning, the bell mule is brought to the line and all the rest follow & take their place by their own saddle. If there happens to be a recruit amongst them who don't understand the ropes & gets in the wrong place, the others bite & kick at him until he finds it. These mules either get to know the number on the saddle or they can remember the identical spot where they were removed. On the march, the keepers ride alongside (of which there is 6 to 50 mules) & if any packs get loose the mule is headed off, the pack tightened & off he goes on a trot to catch his long-eared brethren, who always keep on the move either fast or slow, according to the gait of the bell mule, who is led. The saddles this train uses are not the common pack saddle, but a Mexican invention called *Aparejo*. It's like two large leather cushions hinged together at the top. The way they & the packs are put on is as follows: First, a couple of saddle blankets are put on, then the aparejo is sat astride of the animal's back, when a wide girth is passed around & fastened. These cushions stand from 6 to 8 inches clear of the animal's back & they rest on the upper part of his ribs or side. Now the boxes or sacks are laid on as near the top as possible &

fastened together with a rope so that it bears across the top. Now another very wide & strong girth is passed under the animal with a hook on either end, then a long cord 25 or 30 feet long is thrown across the pack, crossed & recrossed, & each time hooked on the girth or around the corner of the cushions. (These cushions are stiffened with pliable ribs generally made of stout willow boughs.) When this is done they commence to pull the cord, taking out all the slack first, then the cinching begins. They have as much purchase as though they were pulling on tackle. When the pack is secure the mule is let go and another is taken. Those that understand this work fasten on packs very quick. It requires 2 men to work at a pack at a time. The mule stands without being held because he is blindfolded. They have a leather hood which is sat over the ears & it falls down over his eyes. Bags & bundles seldom if ever get loose during the day if time is given to fasten them before starting. It's boxes that they have the most trouble with.[78]

July 21st.

This has been the warmest day of summer, I think. Let the days be ever so warm, it helps the nights but little. One can sleep under 3 woolen blankets without feeling uncomfortable. Steamers are coming up with supplies for Tongue River

---

78. The pack-mule train was a mainstay of the Indian-fighting army. For an overview of its operation, see J. A. Breckons, "The Army Pack Train Service," *Recreation*, 6 (June 1897), 426-28; and Robert A. Murray, "'I'd like to be a Packer': The Role of Mule Trains in the Western Campaigns," *By Valor and Arms, The Journal of American Military History*, 3 (no. 3, 1979), 22-29. For the rudiments and mechanics of the pack train service, see Henry W. Daly, *Manual of Pack Transportation* (Washington, D.C.: Government Printing Office, 1910).

& the Big Horn posts daily, also some miners for the Big
Horn Mountains are to be seen on nearly every boat. The
most of these supplies are sent to Bismarck [via] Northern
Pacific R.R. & from there it's transferred on boats [for ship-
ment upriver to the Montana posts].

" *22nd.*

Weather very warm. This morning a steamer of a medium
size shot by our camp like an arrow. I could scarcely make
out the name. I took it for the *Meadows*[79] of St. Louis. It
must have run at the rate of 30 miles per hour.

" *23rd.*

The weather is getting hot. I don't know as it's any warmer
than some days in Ohio. I think it's the nights being so cold
it makes it feel so uncomfortable.

" *24th.*

Not as warm as yesterday. The steamer *Victor*[80] brought us
16 more pack animals & men to handle them, & about 9
P.M. the steamer *Savannah*[81] brought us some mail & a Gatling

---

79. This vessel was apparently known by another name, not *Meadows*.
80. According to Private Edward Williams, of Company H, this
was the *Fanchon*. "Memorandum of Edward Williams, Company 'H,'
2nd Cavalry, Fort Ellis, M.T., 1876 and 1877," 48, typescript, Little Bighorn Battlefield National Monument, Crow Agency, Montana. There
is no *Victor* listed in *Way's Packet Directory* that operated on the
Yellowstone or Missouri in 1877.
81. The wooden-hulled sternwheel packet *Savannah*, built in Pennsylvania in 1863, originally operated between Pittsburgh and St Louis.
She measured 156 feet by 35 feet and was damaged in an ice gorge in
1876 at St. Louis. In 1881 *Savannah* was renamed *Flying Eagle* but had
apparently been retired by 1884. Ibid., 420.

gun[82] with men & horses. This is a new gun to me. It's a breech loader & a revolver. (There's a crank to it like an organ, but I think it will make rather louder music.) The bore is 2 inch & it throws an explosive bullet. (Later) A little rain is falling on going to bed.

July 25th.

Weather quite pleasant. At 12 M the steamer *Kansas Jo*[83] took us all across to the south side of the Yellowstone again & we are camped exactly where we were one week ago [July 18]. There is another expedition on foot.

" *26th.*

We had a heavy thunder storm today. One day's [supply] of oats was sent to Beaver Creek on packs & a small escort, some of which are to come back with the mules & the balance stay with the grain.

---

82. The "organ-grinding" Gatling gun was perfected during the Civil War by inventor Richard J. Gatling. The weapon, used sparingly during that conflict, saw limited use during the postwar Indian campaigns. Manufactured in three calibers, it was described succinctly as follows: "A machine gun, the 1 inch composed of six and the ½ inch of ten rifled barrels of steel, made to revolve around a central axis parallel to their bores, by means of a hand crank. . . . With each revolution of the crank the 1-inch gun fires once, and the ½-inch gun three times. The ½-inch gun is reduced to calibre .45 inch, in order to use with it the projectile of the breech-loading [Springfield] musket." Thomas Wilhelm, *A Military Dictionary and Gazetteer* (Philadelphia: L. R. Hamersly and Company, 1881), 187.

83. There is no *Kansas Jo* listed in *Way's Packet Directory*. Private Edward Williams's "Memorandum" (p. 48) stated that the *Savannah* arrived on the 25th "and sett [sic] off some Artillery. This morning we all crossed again." It is likely that the *Savannah* transported the troops.

" *27th.*

It's been a cold & rainy day. The boys have been practicing with the little cannon. It's a nice little piece of furniture. It only weighs 400 lbs., & 4 horses which are used on it ought to be able to drag it anywhere.[84]

" *28th.*

Weather very pleasant. We broke up camp early & took our back trail towards Beaver Creek, where we camped on the 8th, & found our boys & oats all right. We are to take up the trail we left on the Little Missouri & follow it or bust.[85]

" *29th.*

Weather fine. We are camped on Beaver Creek near where we camped the 9th. (I gave a description of this region in the fore part of the month.)[86] This evening an infantryman of the 5th came in & gave himself up as a deserter. Said he was going to the Black Hills & lost the way, that he de-

---

84. See footnote 87, below.

85. Wrote Major Brisbin: "On the 28th of July [I] was ordered out with the battalion in pursuit of the same Indians Captain Ball had been following, and struck the trail on the 1st of August. We followed these Indians 22 days, traveling over 400 miles, often camping without wood or water, and eating rations raw. We could not overhaul the Indians, but compelled them to drop their lodges and camp-fixtures, many of their ponies, and forced them to go into Red Cloud agency and surrender. This was one of the hardest marches I ever made, and I doubt if a harder one has been made. The men, at one time, were entirely out of rations, and some of the soldiers without meat for three days. The troops engaged in this service were Captain Ball, H, Captain Tyler, F, and Captain Wheelan, G Companies, Second Cavalry; Captain McDougall, B Company, Seventh Cavalry; Captain Casey, A Company, and First Lieutenant Logan, H Company, Fifth Infantry, mounted. Brisbin to AAGDD, October 26, 1877, in *Report of the Secretary of War, 1877*, 552.

86. See entries for July 4, 9, and 10.

serted from Tongue River Post. He had a horse & rifle but his chuck had run out some time ago. He had killed one deer & was obliged to eat it raw, as he had no means for starting a fire.

July 30th.

Last night we had a terrific thunderstorm such as one can only see in this region, & today it's been quite cool. We stayed in camp till 12 M [waiting] for B Co. of 7th Cavalry & 2 Co. of the 5 Infantry (Mounted) to come up which they did. They started from Powder River near the Yellowstone some time ago. A large train started with them to supply us with rations & they are to follow up in the rear. It has 2 co. of infantry along for guard.[87]

" 31st.

The weather continues cool. We followed our back trail most of the way. Tonight we are camped on a nice spring, with lots of wood. About 2 hours after we got in camp, 46

---

87. On July 22, Miles sent Major Brisbin the following dispatch accounting for the reinforcements mentioned by Zimmer and providing direction for his movements: "I send you at once all the force you ask, and in addition, the best steel rifled gun, in my opinion, in this country for Indian service. [This was a recently acquired Hotchkiss gun, which would be used for the first time in Indian warfare that fall against the Nez Perces at Bear's Paw Mountains.] Major Lazelle has orders to move down to a point near Sentinel Buttes, and will be available to co-operate, furnish supplies, or, if a large force of Indians is found, to join you for any service. Please do all in your power to destroy or drive in that band [refugees from Lame Deer's village], and spare neither horseflesh or pains to accomplish the work. When the commands turn west or back, should the Indians retreat toward the head of the Powder River, I wish the grass burned behind you in the whole section of country, and the region of the Little Missouri left unsuitable for Indians or game." *Army and Navy Journal,* July 22, 1877.

Crow Indians & 6 squaws came in from Doane's camp in charge of a soldier of G Co. with a half-breed squaw for interpreter by the name of Emma Shean.[88] Her father has been government interpreter at the Crow Agency for the last 20 years.

To be continued

There's only 5 months in this, as I have got tired of copying.[89] I will send the other 7 [sic—5] months some other time.

---

88. Emma Shane, or Chien, or Chienne, was a mixed-blood daughter of Pierre Chien, an agent of the American Fur Company, and his Crow wife, Bear in the Woods. Pierre Chien had lived with the Mountain Crows since the 1840s, had interpreted for them at councils since the 1860s, and later became interpreter at the Crow Agency. Joseph Medicine Crow, *From the Heart of Crow Country: The Crow Indians' Own Stories* (New York: Orion Books, 1992), 50-52; Hoxie, *Parading through History*, 91.

89. This remark confirms that the present diary was transcribed by Zimmer from a likely original, thereby accounting for comments that were subsequently interjected into this generation of the document.

PART TWO

～

August 1, 1877, to December 31, 1877
Conclusion of the Sioux Campaign,
the Nez Perce Campaign, and After

August 1st.

Weather pleasant. About 4 P.M. we reached the Little Missouri River, where we left the Sioux trail on the 14th of July. After crossing and going up a mile we went in camp for the night.[1] We had not been in camp but a short time when 66 more Crow warriors came to us down the numerous ravines that lead to the river, in single file with their feathers flying and they yelling like fiends of Hell.[2] They were in charge of an infantry officer. They went in camp along with the other Indians that came to us last night. After supper had been got away with, about one

---

1. This was in present Slope County, North Dakota.

2. On July 28, a hundred Crows had been sent by steamboat to the mouth of Glendive Creek to accompany the troops en route to the Little Missouri country, where the Sioux were expected to be. *Bozeman Times*, August 9, 1877.

hundred Indians mounted their ponies, first having fixed
their toilets in war paint, and adorned their head and hair
with feathers. Also, the mane and tail of their ponies, and
those having white ponies (which are very plenty amongst
them) they daub red paint on so as to look as though they
had been wounded. They formed a half-mile ring around
our camp and began to ride on a brisk trot, at the same
time singing and shouting at the top of their voices, and
those that were not mounted stood in groups around the
ring indulging in the same kind of vocal music. They have
no flags, but long stained rods on which they have long
streamers of feathers. On some there is scalps cut in long
strips, with the hair hanging and fluttering in the breeze as
they rode around at the same time swinging their rifles,
tomahawks or knives over their heads in a fantastic man-
ner. They kept this up for half an hour, then going to their
camp they commenced their medicine making, which they
kept up until 12 midnight. This war dance or jamboree
which I have been trying to explain, would beat Barnum's
Hippodrome all to pieces.[3] Their war headdresses are made
in different styles, but the most common are a buckskin
turban, streamers of the same which hang nearly down to
the ground. The outside of the turban is beaded, & in the
inside the feathers are fastened in an upright position. On
the streamers, they are fastened in such a way so as to flutter
when they are riding fast. (The Indians in the Muddy Creek
[Lame Deer] fight had no time to display their fine headdresses. There was lots of them there and very fine ones
which were all destroyed.) The feathers that are principally

---

3. The reference is to showman Phineas T. Barnum's circus, "The
Greatest Show on Earth," which had entertained crowds since 1871.

used are those of the eagle and wild turkey. Indians are very fond of bright and gaudy colors, and if they see any trinket which they like they will have it regardless of cost, if they have the price of it in their possession. And jewelry they all wear. Of course, it's nothing but brass or German silver. Some of them will have a cord around their necks filled with all kinds of stuff just so it shines. I have seen some with rings on all of their fingers—not only one on a finger, but 3 and 4 on each. And for earrings, it's awful. They will be from 2 to 2½ inches across and from 3 to 4 in each ear, one above the other. And the holes in the outer edge of their ears are as large as an eyelet in a shoe. Besides the weight of these rings, they have from 2 to 3 ounces of trinkets, such as fancy little shells, elk tusks, and large beads, all suspended from their ears. (Perhaps it would be as well here to give you their mode of dress. On their feet they wear moccasins altogether, either made of buffalo or deer-skin, according to the weather. On their body they wear a shirt, leggins & a breechclout. Then, according to the se-verity of the weather, they either wear a blanket or a robe about the body. Their heads are generally bare. They are more apt to buy a hat of the trader to keep the sun off, than a cap for winter use. The squaws seldom ever wear any-thing else than a piece of calico about their heads. Their bodily dress is much the same as the male, with an addi-tional short skirt made of a blanket. In fact, all their wear-ing apparel is made of blankets except shirts, which are invariably red flannel. They would go to Hell after a red blanket if they couldn't get it outside. The way the leggins are made is this: They take a piece of blanket wide enough to leave a selvage 4 inches wide on the outside of the leg, which is cut into fringe. They sometimes make a ghastly

looking cloak with a hood to it, which they fringe wher-
ever they can put it on. They never pretend to wash anything in the clothing line, though they are quite fond of
bathing when the water is warm. Yet I doubt whether they
do it for cleanliness. I rather think it's done for coolness.)[4]

August 2nd.

Weather fair. After following the trail 12 miles we came out
on a beautiful prairie well watered with small streams &
basins. These streams and basins, or ponds, are alive with all
size and colors of ducks. This is a great breeding place for
them, as one can see hundreds of young ones unable to fly.
As small as the cannon is, it gave us some trouble this forenoon. Before the Crow Indians came to us, we had 5 [or?]
6 Cheyenne Indians from Tongue River, and last night they
failed to come in. The Crows either scared them away or
they took their hair, as they did those at Tongue River last
winter.[5] We are camped tonight on a nice running brook
with wood plenty.

---

4. The Crows took great pride in their individual appearance and
devoted great attention to it. Their clothing and ornamentation was
consequently of major importance, with men wearing shell earrings,
feathered headdresses, leggings, breechcloths, and shirts, much as described by Zimmer. For particulars of Crow dress, see Josephine Paterek,
Encyclopedia of American Indian Costume (New York: W. W. Norton and
Company, 1994), 107–11; and Lowie, *Crow Indians*, 81–84. Contrary to
Zimmer's opinion, the Crows bathed frequently for personal cleanliness and spiritual purposes. Ibid., 89–90.

5. The reference is to the ambush killing, by Crow scouts, of five
Teton leaders as they approached the Tongue River Cantonment to
inquire about peace terms on December 16, 1876. The incident threw
Colonel Miles's hopes for ending the warfare into a quandary and likely
contributed to extending the army conflict with the Sioux. See Greene,
Yellowstone Command, 147–52.

August 3rd.

Weather fine. Country rolling prairie. Water good and plenty, wood only in long distances and then scarce. This morning all but 40 of the Indians were sent back, as we had not enough rations for them. About noon we lost the trail. They have scattered in search of game. Antelope are plenty. (We still kept in the direction of their trail, hoping to find it.) Tonight we are camped on a stream that is supposed to be Knife River.[6] Today we crossed the Cannonball River. They are both small this season of the year, and up here they haven't the appearance of ever being large. On Knife River where we are camped there isn't a sign of wood, so we are obliged to go to sleep without eating anything warm.

" *4th.*

The weather had been very warm. We left camp without any breakfast in search of wood & the lost trail. About noon we found a little brush wood on a brook where we went in camp for the day. The country has been very fine, antelope & feathered game plenty. (The Indians are about camp in Adam & Eve style.)

August 5th.

Weather very fine. This morning 40 men were detailed to go in search of the train, as our rations were nearly gone. (I amongst the number.) We went to our right, in the direction of the upper Little Missouri, for there the train could

---

6. Zimmer's identification of this stream as Knife River is wrong, and probably reflects the geographical vagaries of the country as understood by many of the enlisted men. Most likely they were camped on an affluent of Cedar Creek in present Slope County, North Dakota.

only cross. Water & sometimes wood was plenty up to 3 P.M. After that it began to grow scarce. When we wanted to go in camp, there was no wood, so we kept on, hoping to find both, until 9 P.M. Here we found wood but no water. We could go no further, for it was so dark one couldn't see a hole in the ground. So we were obliged to eat hard bread & fried bacon, which only increased our thirst. The men groped up and down the ravine in the brush in hopes to find some water, but all in vain.

" *6th.*

It's been a very warm day. Everyone was stirring about camp by 3 A.M. (as dry as a fish, the saying is) and in half an hour we were on our way without breakfast. Everyone cared more for drinking just now. Whenever we came to a hollow or ravine, men would be sent in search of water, and yet none was found at [by] 9 A.M. About this time we saw the train on a distant hill about 15 miles off. Here the country became very rough and anyone would suppose that some water should be found, but we were obliged to go an hour longer, when we found some passable alkali water. At this time we & the horses hadn't drank any for nearly 24 hours, not because we couldn't, but because we thought it being so plenty it would last, so not even a man had any in his canteen on account of its getting so much warmer than it already is in this season of the year. I thought the horses would hurt themselves drinking. They acted as though they would never stop. I have often went 24 hours without tasting but little water, in fact had but little desire to, but this time my desire had been greatly enlarged. It may be, because we couldn't get it, [it] made our minds dwell on it the more. We unsaddled at the water's edge, hobbled our horses and ate breakfast. We stayed

XXXII and the oather 3 foloued up in the rear. We ar to make for a yndian camp somewhere in the neighborhood of the Rosebud (This is not the Rosebud River that the Crow Agency is on) By 6 P m we reachd the Rosebud a very narrow & crooked stream the bank ar thickly coverd with ash & wilow & the Banks ar so steep that crossing is very dificult, bsids its full of quick Sand We folowed up the River a short distance (by this time it was pitch Dark but still we kep on our way) then turnd up to our right amongst the hills towards the Big Horn this we never halted till 5 am the morning of the 6th May. 6th Weather plesant after the halt we fed our horses an extry dose & had breakfast, then the Scouts wer sent out of which we had 4 2 half Breeds & 2 yndians in an hours time they wer back & soon after we wer off again up a small stream with a beautiful bottom & nicely sloping hills coverd with green grass & shrubery (the creek has all kinds of wild fruit on it such as Plumms currents cheries Gooseberies & strawberies & they ar all in full Bloom giving the air a beatiful smell, also anoather lot of new flowers ar puting in theair appearance) we hadent gon far before we came to an yndian camping place, it having ben diserted only a few days before. this is the place where they wer campd when the Scouts

A sample page of Zimmer's journal

here until 1 P.M., when we started after the train, which was going in the right direction, but slow. The best of the country is rough & in places barren. They went in camp about 5 P.M. & shortly after we came up. They were camped in a woodless country but they had several wagons loaded with it for emergency. (We have 20 pack mules along which I forgot to mention, and before leaving our breakfast place we loaded 4 of them with wood.)

August 7th.
Weather warm. We stayed in camp 2 hours after the train left & overtook them by noon. Then our 20 mules were packed & by 3 P.M. were on our way to the command, leaving the train to follow our trail at leisure. (The train went in camp here for the night.) We soon struck the trail that we made two days ago & by 9 P.M. found the command where we had left them, without food enough for breakfast in the morning.

August 8th.
Weather pleasant. The 3 cos. of cav. started on to where the scouts had found a faint trail. We did not leave camp until 12 M & got there at 4 P.M. The infantry are to remain & wait for the train & follow up. We have no wood this evening, so we are again euchred out of a warm supper. The country is not as good as it has been. It is hillier & the ground is covered with stone & the grass is short. Grass is not as good anywhere now as it was a month ago.

" 9th.
Weather & country the same as yesterday. We left camp early & camped at the first wood & water. This was found

at 1 P.M. The water is very good, the wood is nothing but wild cherry brush & rose bushes, few at that.

" *10th.*

Weather fine. In a few miles we came to an old Indian camp. From here the trail increased in size & in a few miles we came to another camping place & the trail again increased. The country kept growing worse until it became the worst kind of badland. In time this turned to a rocky, mountainous region dotted with pines & fir trees. We traveled in this a short time, when the little gun horses & driver were upset down a bank some distance, breaking the pole, but fortunately no one was hurt. The trail soon ran down on a level prairie and here a great number of Indians had camped for some time. (The Crow Indians say there was somewhere in the neighborhood of 300 & that they didn't leave that camp more than 4 days ago.) From here the trail circled around the prairie a few miles, then it took through a rocky range & by a place known by the military as Slim Buttes. We went but a short distance further, where we found some bad water and lots of wood & went in camp. Here where we are camped Colonel Mills had a skirmish with Crazy Horse's band last fall a year & lost 2 men.[7] Just

---

7. The Battle of Slim Buttes occurred on September 9–10, 1876. Captain Anson Mills, of Crook's field command, was en route to the Black Hills mining settlements for supplies with 150 men of the Third Cavalry when he happened on a village of Sioux and Northern Cheyennes. These people had been in the Powder River country and were presently camped within the boundaries of the Great Sioux Reservation. Attacking at dawn, the soldiers drove the Indians from their camp. The warriors returned with reinforcements in the afternoon, but Crook's force, which had reached the scene in the interim, successfully repelled the tribesmen. Army casualties numbered three killed and twenty-four

as we were passing Slim Buttes the sun was setting over their peaks, & the scene was delightful. Before we reached the badlands we crossed a stream called Grand River. I didn't see anything grand about it. It had scarcely water enough to give our horses a drink & not a sprig of wood grew along its banks. Its channel is very wide & it's likely some seasons of the year a great quantity of water flows down.

August 11th.

Weather fine. Early this morning two scouts were sent back to meet the balance of our command & the train to guide them a newer and better way to us than what the trail ran, & if that can't be done, for them to send us some supplies on packs, as we only took enough for 5 days. We stayed in camp all day.

August 12th.

Weather fine. Early this morning I went back to have a good look at the buttes.[8] They are beautiful. The more one

----

wounded; the Indians lost about ten killed and two wounded. See Jerome A. Greene, *Slim Buttes, 1876: An Episode of the Great Sioux War* (Norman: University of Oklahoma Press, 1982). Anson Mills (1834–1924), a native of Indiana, attended West Point for two years, but entered the Civil War an enlisted man. He was quickly commissioned in the Eighteenth Infantry, however, and fought at, among other places, Stone's River, Tennessee; Chickamauga and Atlanta, Georgia; and Nashville, Tennessee, being wounded once and breveted three times. In the postwar army, Mills transferred to the Third Cavalry, with which unit he served until 1878. He served successively in the Tenth Cavalry, Fourth Cavalry, and, again, Third Cavalry. He retired as brigadier general in 1897, and authored *My Story* (Washington, D.C.: Byron S. Adams, 1918). Carroll and Price, *Roll Call on the Little Big Horn*, 144.

8. The Slim Buttes consist of a low-lying range of pastel-colored clay and limestone pinnacles running approximately twenty miles north to south and six miles east to west. They are located about twenty miles

looks at them the more attractive they become. For about 100 feet, the base, which is perpendicular, are of a mixed color pink & cream. Then, from a horizontal line, the rock is nearly white & in a rugged shape, yet keeping its full size for 30 feet. Then the color changes to black, & three or four steeple-shaped spires run up for a number of feet further, & in several places small pines have taken root. This is the description of the three largest ones as near as I can give. There is a number of smaller ones near by, which I will let pass. Besides these buttes, the scene is very fine. Later, the command & train reached us at noon. They found a very good pass around the east end of the badlands. By 3 P.M. the mules were packed with all the rations in the train and we moved on. (The train and 2 cos. of infantry that came with the train have returned to the Yellowstone River.) The scene all the afternoon were grand. This evening we are camped on some pools of very bad water, there being a green scum over the whole surface. Wood & grass is plenty.

" *13th.*

Weather fair. The trail ran through a poor &, in places, barren prairie, yet well watered, but no wood. We traveled so far in the night, in hopes to find both, that we couldn't find water enough for the stock, but wood was plenty. Indians had camped here a few days ago & the water had since dried up. This is in the edge of another range of rocky hills. The grass is fair.

---

east of present Buffalo, South Dakota. For a full description, see John Paul Gries, *Roadside Geology of South Dakota* (Missoula, Mont.: Mountain Press Publishing Company, 1996), 153–56.

August 14th.

Weather fair. We left camp early & by 9 A.M. found another Indian camp, or rather where they had camped, & a splendid spring of water. Here we stayed 4 hours, stabled out the horses, & cooked dinner. After dinner we started again & traveled until 5 P.M. to another Indian camping place with plenty of wood & water. We pass from 2 to 3 Indian camping [sites] per day, but whether they stay overnight in each or not is unknown. If they do stay in each overnight, we must be gaining on them fast. The country has been hilly & rocky all day, with lots of pine in the ravines.

" *15th.*

Weather fair. For a few hours the trail kept in the same kind of country as yesterday. Then it ran down on a prairie & by noon we came on the Little Missouri River again, way up where one can find places to walk across without getting one's feet wet with shoes on. We followed up the bottom, first crossing then re-crossing a number of times, until night. Large timber is scarce & the grass is very poor. The soil is heavy clay & in places there's nothing growing, not even prickly pear.

August 16th.

Weather fair. The trail kept up the river until 11 A.M. Here we stopped and ate dinner, then took up the trail again, which turned due west, towards Powder River. We went in this direction about 8 miles, when we came to another camping place of theirs. Here we went in camp for the night. We passed but one of their camps today, & in it, as well as the one we are in, there's lots of refuse of a plundered wagon train, very likely some miners' outfit, as we are but 60 miles from the Black Hills mines. Two men of B Co., 7th Cav. skipped for the hills last night.[9] One of the Crow Indians has been bitten by a rattler & his leg is swollen very bad, besides it makes him very sick. He binds on some kind of weed. This is the first case of a rattlesnake bite I've heard of, as plenty as they are. The country is very poor, [with] scarcely any grass but lots of sagebrush & prickly pears. This Indian camp that we are in tonight is on a tributary of the Little Missouri. Wood is not plenty.

August 17th.
Weather fair. The fore part of the day was like yesterday. Near night it became hilly & broken, also well-timbered for these parts. Here the little cannon got another downfall & she is now a total wreck. The caisson is still drawn by horses, but the cannon & its fixtures are on mules. Tonight we are camped on a small stream amongst the hills & it's supposed to be the head of Glendive Creek.[10]

" *18th.*
Weather very warm. The Indians have been riding along in a naked state. The country until evening has been like that of yesterday evening. This evening we are camped amongst sagebrush & prickly pears, & the horses have poor picking.

---

9. The Black Hills gold rush occurred between 1874 and 1879. It coincided with a generally depressed national economy and drew wide attention, including that of troops operating in the region in 1877, and numerous desertions took place. For full particulars of the rush, see Watson Parker, *Gold in the Black Hills* (Norman: University of Oklahoma Press, 1966).

10. The identity of this stream is unknown, but it was most likely not Glendive Creek.

We found some water, but we are obliged to burn sage-brush for wood.

August 19th.
Weather warm. The country has been very poor, but level. This evening we are camped on a creek that empties in Powder River, where grazing is better.

" *20th.*
Weather very cold. We had a heavy thunder & rain storm last night which has greatly changed the weather from that of yesterday. Everyone that had an overcoat along wore it until noon, when it moderated some. We followed the trail down the creek to Powder River. Here we went in camp on a nice bottom where grass is quite good. Powder River here at this time of year is 3 rods wide, water 14 inches deep, clear & good.

" *21st.*
Weather milder. The trail left the river & took a northwest direction across a high but quite level country, sometimes through groves of pine & cedar. This evening we are camped on a creek that runs back to Powder River. This water is the pure tincture of alkali. It's as red as blood. Wood is plenty.

" *22nd.*
The weather is warmer than yesterday, though we had quite a shower last night. We followed the trail but a short distance when it became invisible. They had scattered again, but before doing so they threw away all dispensable stuff, such as lodge poles, camp kettles, & various other truck too numerous to describe. Sioux Indians were seen several times

in small parties on high knolls, but by the time our men got there they were somewhere else. (You might as well hunt a needle in a haystack, as to hunt Indians in small parties.) After the trail was no more, we turned toward Powder River, where we expect to meet rations, as we have but two days [worth yet available] after today. This evening we are camped on a small stream the scouts say is a fork of Powder River. Grass, wood & alkali water plenty. The country has been very rolling all day with grazing in abundance.

August 23rd.

Weather same as yesterday. We followed the stream down to its junction with Powder River. Its banks are thickly covered with willows & cottonwood, & the valley very narrow. At times we were obliged to go up on the tableland. We are camped on a nice grassy bottom, but we can't see anything of that expected outfit (with our grub—that's troubling us the most right now) that was to meet us here. A half-breed was sent to Tongue River Post while we were yet on the upper waters of the Little Missouri River to let them know of our condition & to send supplies to this place, and for fear that the first messenger could not get through, the second one was sent the night after. Major Brisbin issued an order to the quartermaster this evening, that if rations did not reach us before ours ran out, that good, fat horses & mules should be slaughtered and given out. He also advised everyone to eat hearty of them, saying that it was good and wholesome [even] if the Americans had not adopted it yet as an article of food. That is if it should come to this, but he hoped not & thought that the morrow would bring the hash. If it don't we will make hash of the mules.

August 24th.

Weather cool. A party was sent ahead to look up our rations, as ours play out tonight, & permission was given everyone that wanted to go hunting, just so they would return at noon, for at this time we were to move downstream. About noon the boys began to come in with a variety of game, such as deer, antelope, rabbits, prairie dogs & chickens. Yet this was rather a small supply when we look at the number there is to eat them. Game is very scarce just as we want them, & have been for some days past. We left our camp at the appointed time. The river bottoms are of the nicest kind, well timbered along the river bank & grass. This afternoon we passed the wreck of a wagon train. I found out that it belonged to a government surveying party & that they got snowed in in September 1870 & while they were in this fix the Indians pounced on them and they were obliged to retreat to the Yellowstone. But before doing so, seeing they could not move their train, they shot their mules & burnt their train. (Someone has placed all the mules' heads in a row at the edge of the timber which are now bleached as white as snow & I should think there is 40 of them.) This party was composed of the engineers & 2 cos. of infantry. The Indians kept following them up in their retreat & shooting in the rear of their column every morning. The snow did not last long, so one morning they left camp earlier than they were use to doing & secreted one co. in the willows & as soon as the Indians had passed them they followed on as much secreted as possible until they were within shooting distance of the advance co. when both cos. let loose on them & killed some 30 without having a single one killed on the soldiers' side, but some wounded.

The Indians took to the hills & were seen no more. I give you this as I heard it.[11] Evening came at last & we went in camp & the party that went in search of the rations have not returned yet. So I think we are out of luck for a heavy breakfast in the morning.

August 25th.

Weather nice & cool. We broke camp very early & started down the river (for it didn't take long to get away with the 3 hardtack we got apiece of the infantry companies who had yet a few on hand & who were kind enough to share with us). The party that went out yesterday in search of the rations returned during the night. About 11 A.M. we met 2 white couriers who brought us some mail & orders to leave the trail. Here we first heard of Gibbon's fight with the Nez Perces which done so little good & yet

---

11. The troops with Zimmer had stumbled upon remnants from the 1865 army command of Colonel Nelson Cole of Brigadier General Patrick E. Connor's Powder River Expedition against the Teton Sioux, Northern Cheyennes, and Arapahoes. Cole's column, beset by early September with bad luck, insufficient rations, Indian attacks, and alternately scorching and freezing temperatures that killed hundreds of its starved and exhausted animals along the Powder, had to abandon and destroy much of its equipment and withdraw upstream in the direction of Fort Connor in Wyoming Territory, fighting the Indians most of the way. The troops, aided by artillery fire, were constrained to withdraw defensively until September 20, when they reached the post. For a comprehensive documentary treatment of the expedition, see LeRoy R. Hafen and Ann W. Hafen, eds., *Powder River Campaigns and Sawyers Expedition of 1865* (Glendale, Calif.: Arthur H. Clark Company, 1961). Concise syntheses appear in Brigham D. Madsen, *Glory-Hunter: A Biography of Patrick Edward Connor* (Salt Lake City: University of Utah Press, 1990), 138–54; and Robert M. Utley, *Frontiersmen in Blue: The United States Army and the Indian, 1848–1865* (New York: The Macmillan Company, 1967), 322–31.

had 53 men killed or wounded.[12] We also learned that our rations started 3 days before these men did, & that they went up Tongue River & expected to cross over after getting up a ways, so we started to meet them. Taking across

---

12. At dawn on August 9, 1877, Colonel John Gibbon, commander of the Military District of Montana, attacked a camp of approximately 800 Nez Perce Indians, including 125 warriors, along the Big Hole River in southwestern Montana Territory. The nontreaty Nez Perces, led by Joseph, Looking Glass, White Bird, and others, had crossed the Bitterroot Mountains from Idaho Territory following several engagements with the troops of Brigadier General Oliver O. Howard, commanding the Military Department of the Columbia. Formerly friendly tribesmen, the Nez Perces had taken up arms in the face of mounting pressures: the continuing encroachment onto their traditional lands by white settlers, demands that they move onto a reservation, and frustrations from seeing their friends and relatives killed with impunity by whites. They soon fled Idaho, and the army gave chase, catching the Nez Perces at the Big Hole River. Gibbon, a Civil War veteran officer with much experience in the West (see below), led a column composed of Seventh infantrymen, Second cavalrymen (from Zimmer's regiment), and volunteers, surprising the Nez Perce village at dawn and inflicting substantial casualties. The tribesmen, however, recovered from the assault and struck back, laying siege to Gibbon's troops over the next day before finally withdrawing from the area. Gibbon's command suffered casualties of twenty-nine killed and forty wounded (including Gibbon), while the Nez Perces lost between sixty and ninety dead, mostly women, children, and old men. The Indians moved south and east, largely eluding Howard's pursuing army before passing through Yellowstone National Park and then heading north, ultimately trying to reach Canada. On September 30, Colonel Nelson A. Miles attacked the Nez Perces near the Bear's Paw Mountains in northern Montana. Five days later they surrendered. Zimmer was on hand for the battle and surrender. The most complete account of Gibbon's engagement is in Aubrey L. Haines, *An Elusive Victory: The Battle of the Big Hole* (West Glacier, Mont.: Glacier Natural History Association, 1991). On the Nez Perces, see Alvin M. Josephy, Jr., *The Nez Perce Indians and the Opening of the Northwest* (New Haven: Yale University Press, 1965); and for the Nez Perce War, see Mark H. Brown, *The Flight of the Nez Perce* (New York: Capricorn Books, 1971). The Nez Perce perspective on these events is presented in Lucullus V. McWhorter, *Yellow Wolf: His Own*

the hills towards Tongue River, we had been on the way about 2 hours when 2 Cheyenne Indians overtook us. They had come from the party we were looking for. They said our rations were up the river where they had orders to guide them & that they were coming down on our trail. So we turned back to the [Powder] river & went in camp & some Indians were sent back up the river to have them make as much haste as possible & get down to us. We waited & waited & would have went hungry to bed only for the infantry. They gave us 4 hardtack apiece & some coffee, but no sugar. About 11 P.M. 2 cos. of the 7th Cavalry & a few pack mules came in. They had left the wagon train over at Tongue River, as they were unable to bring it across the hills.[13] The country along the river today was as good if not better than yesterday.

Story (Caldwell, Idaho: The Caxton Printers, Ltd., 1940); and Lucullus V. McWhorter, *Hear Me, My Chiefs! Nez Perce History and Legend*, ed. Ruth Bordin (Caldwell, Idaho: The Caxton Printers, Ltd., 1952).

John Gibbon (1827–1896) graduated from West Point in 1847. He served against the Seminoles in Florida before becoming an instructor in artillery at the Military Academy (he authored *The Artillerist's Manual*, published in 1863). During the Civil War he successively became a brigade, division, and corps commander, leading commands at South Mountain and Antietam, Maryland; and Spotsylvania and Petersburg, Virginia. Wounded at Fredericksburg, Virginia, and Gettysburg, Pennsylvania, Gibbon was a major general by 1864. The postwar reorganization of the army found him a colonel of the Seventh Infantry by 1869, in which command he played important roles in both the Sioux campaign that culminated in Custer's disaster and the Nez Perce War. Promoted to brigadier general in 1885, Gibbon retired from the service six years later. He died in 1896. Heitman, *Historical Register and Dictionary*, 1:452. For various of his writings, see John Gibbon, *Adventures on the Western Frontier*, ed. Alan and Maureen Gaff (Bloomington: Indiana University Press, 1994), which includes his account of the Big Hole encounter, 203–18.

13. The supply train, sent out from Tongue River Cantonment on August 21, was escorted by Companies H, D, and K, Seventh Cavalry, and Companies B and F (mounted), and C (foot), Fifth Infantry, com-

August 26th.

Weather cool. We stayed in this camp all day. The rations were issued in due time for breakfast this morning. So we escaped eating horsemeat this time.

" 27th.

Weather warm. We started early for Tongue River & to wagons, yet we made but a short march as we went in camp at 1 P.M. On the march, the rear guard had instructions to set fire to the grass as we went along. I don't know why this is done, except it's to prevent hostile Indians from camping in this part of the country the coming winter. After we went in camp the Indians [scouts] kept on, they having been promised of having their ponies shod as soon as they reached the train. The Indians' stock is all played out, they have either sore backs or hoof sore. As little as they are rode they won't stand one-fourth as much as an American horse. The Indians have from 3 to 4 ponies each. Where we are camped there is lots of wood & water. Also grass, but it's very dry. Later. The Indians have been setting fires in our advance, either accidental or on purpose, thinking they were doing right. 50 men have been sent to fight it to keep it out of our camp, which it is threatening.[14]

---

manded by Captain Simon Snyder, Fifth Infantry. Major George Gibson to AAGDD, October 1, 1877, in *Report of the Secretary of War, 1877,* 546. These troops, wrote Major Brisbin, "came to our relief on Powder River, as we were out of rations and about to kill horses for food." Brisbin to AAGDD, October 26, 1877, in ibid., 553.

14. Obviously, the burnings by the troops were meant to destroy the grass upon which game—particularly buffalo—and Indian ponies could graze, thus precluding Sioux-Cheyenne use of these traditional hunting lands during the late summer and fall while promoting the necessity of their going into the agencies for survival (See Miles's order

Major James S. Brisbin, Commander of the Second Cavalry Battalion in 1877.
MONTANA HISTORICAL SOCIETY PHOTOGRAPH ARCHIVES, HELENA

---

of July 22 in part 1, footnote 87.) On the other hand, the Indians themselves customarily set fires to impede the army's progress, as well as to
insure new growth in the spring and also, possibly, to control the buffalo
range area. See Hyde, *Red Cloud's Folk*, 274; and telegram, Lieutenant
Colonel James W. Forsyth to Lieutenant General Philip H. Sheridan,
August 6, 1876, Item 5287, RG 393, Records of the Military Division
of the Missouri, NA.

" *28th.*

Weather still warm. The fire was kept out of our camp. After dark it was a beautiful sight which I have longed to see. The wolves made an awful row all night. They howled like fiends of Hell in all directions. We made another early start and camped again at 1 P.M. on a creek that is called Pumpkin Creek. The water is good & wood plenty. The grass is getting quite dry, but in length I haven't seen it beat in my life. It's as tall as rye & stands thick on the ground. I think 5 tons to the acre might be cut here. It isn't so only in a small space, but for miles up & down the creek which has a very wide bottom.

August 29th.

Weather very warm. We made another early start & by 2 P.M. reached Tongue River & the wagons. Setting the grass on fire was continued. The country between Tongue River & Pumpkin Creek is much hillier than that between Powder River & Pumpkin Creek. This evening there is 14 companies, 7 of cavalry & 7 of mounted infantry, besides the Indians.

" *30th.*

Weather windy & cool. The cavalry & infantry that came with the train have returned to the post, leaving us 5 days' rations & oats to get down with. We are to make short marches & let our horses recruit [recuperate]. We started late & went in camp at 4 P.M. The river is low & clear. Grass in great quantities, but quite dry, & we have to be very careful in making fires not to get it on fire & burn our tents up. (I gave a description of this river and country in May. [See entries for May 2, 3, and 4.])

" *31st.*

Weather cloudy & cool. We traveled but a few hours this morning, then went in camp. We passed several haymaking camps of the post quartermaster. Some are cutting with machines & others with scythes & it's being hauled to the post as soon as it is cured. It's only 12 miles to the Yellowstone River now.

September 1st.

Weather fair. We broke camp at noon & moved down within a few miles of the post where grazing is quite good. We received some mail & heard of L Co. having a fight with the Nez Perces in Idaho sometime in August. (Company L of our battalion started from Tongue River the first of July for the National Park with Gens. Sherman & Sheridan. By the time they reached Ft. Ellis the Nez Perce trouble had commenced & they were sent at once to the scene of trouble.)[15]

" *2nd.*

Weather pleasant. Remained in camp all day.

---

15. On July 17, Company L, Second Cavalry, Captain Randolph Norwood commanding, departed the Tongue River Cantonment for Fort Ellis, to escort Commanding General William T. Sherman's party (which did not include Sheridan) into Yellowstone National Park. After Gibbon's battle with the Nez Perces at Big Hole, August 9–10, Company L was diverted to support him and, subsequently, Brigadier General Oliver O. Howard, in pursuit of those Indians. On the night of August 19–20, the unit was camped with Howard's command at Camas Meadows, in Idaho Territory just west of Yellowstone National Park, when the Nez Perces surprised the bivouac and drove off 150 mules and horses. Norwood's men pursued the Indians, were eventually flanked by them, and fought a four-hour engagement until relieved by Howard. Company L returned to Fort Ellis on August 29. Field Returns, Battalion Second Cavalry, July and August, 1877, NAMP M744, Roll 166.

" *3rd.*

Weather pleasant. Still in the same camp.

" *4th.*

Weather & things in general as yesterday.

" *5th.*

Weather the same. Gen. Miles came across the river & inspected our horses & thinks they will soon be able to start on another trip. Quite a number of horses have played out & have been left along our route for the wolves to polish their bones. Since we left Glendive Creek I think B Co. of the 7th Cavalry lost the most.

" *6th.*

Weather very warm this forenoon. This afternoon it began to sprinkle, which cooled the air, but little rain fell.

" *7th.*

Weather cooler.

" *8th.*

Weather fine.

" *9th.*

Weather fine. We moved across Tongue River & up the Yellowstone where we were camped July 3rd.

" *10th.*

Weather very warm. Our boys went fishing with a draw net [seine] (which they borrowed at the post) & caught a large quantity of all kind of fish except trout.

" *11th.*

Weather very cool, caused by a wind storm we had last night.

September 12th.

Weather cool & very windy.

" *13th.*

Weather very cool. The wind nearly blows one's hair off our heads. I was down to Miles City. It has improved wonderful. There is about 20 log houses there now & more underway, besides quite a number of tents. Out of one a doctor has his shingle hung. Another one has the sign of Literature & Stationery. There is now 5 or 6 drinking places & stores, besides a dance house. This is the life of the place in the evenings. As I did not go down in the evening to see the performance, I can only give it to you as I heard it described. The room is quite large with a bar at one side to sell drinks or cigars, which are nothing less than 25 cts. At the end of the room there is 3 musicians perched on a platform of barrels. After quite a crowd gathers in there, which there soon is after working hours, the band begins to play. (These dance houses are very plenty out west. In fact, nearly every town has one or two.) The class of people that attend them the most are miners, mule & ox drivers, wood choppers & gamblers. Sometimes some of those that are looked at as upper tens [upper class] out here go in & take a whirl around for curiosity's sake. At the given time the floor manager shouts out the name of the dance & in a short time the places are all filled. Then the script is taken in, which is 50 cts for each dance. After this the band plays flew con flew [?] as the dancers go whirling around the room. If it's not a round dance they can only dance 2 sets, as they have but 10 ladies, & while 8 are dancing the other 2 are left to entertain the crowd. After each dance, drinks are called up for yourself & partner which is 50 cts more, & if you are anyways backwards in coming forward, your lady partner will tell you in a business way that she is very dry & that the dance has fatigued her greatly. And so it goes, dance after dance & drink after drink, as long as there is men enough to fill a set.

September 14th.
Weather cool. Four men were sent from each company to Ft. Ellis to help the gardeners to harvest the gardens.

" *15th.*
Weather cold & drizzly most of the day. Walters[16] of H Co. drowned in the Yellowstone River while trying to find a fording place. His horse got foundered in quicksand, which caused him to dismount, & while in this condition his horse, plunging to free himself, hurt Walters in some way so that he was unable to swim ashore. Several of his comrades narrowly escaped his fate.

" *16th.*
Weather cooler. We were ferried across the Yellowstone this afternoon. We are to follow the Nez Perces who have crossed the Yellowstone & are making for the Musselshell River.[17]

---

16. Private Frank Walters had enlisted May 10, 1875, in Cincinnati, Ohio. Muster Roll, Company H, Second Cavalry, June 30, 1877–August 31, 1877, RG 94, RAMR, NA.

17. Zimmer, probably writing after the fact here, is confused regarding the purpose of the movement across the Yellowstone on September 16. Although the Nez Perces, ultimately, were to figure predominantly in his unit's attention over the next few weeks, on September 16, Companies

" *17th.*
Weather cool. Last night it froze quite hard. Our course
was north all day, the country has been rolling & grass poor.
This evening we are camped on Sunday Creek. It empties
in the Yellowstone and its waters are alkali. Wood is plenty.
We have a small train with us & 20 days' rations. General
Miles is coming on after us with all the troops that he can
spare from the post as soon as he can load the trains & ferry
everything across.[18]

September 18th.
Weather cool. The country was very poor, sagebrush & prickly
pears plenty in some places. We saw some buffalo in the distance but none were shot. This evening we were unable to
find any wood of any kind, & water is very scarce & poor.
We gathered enough buffalo chips to cook supper with.

" *19th.*
The weather & country was like that of yesterday. Saw lots
of buffalo & antelope. 3 of the former were killed. More

F, G, and H, Second Cavalry, were directed to proceed to Fort Benton
to escort department commander Brigadier General Alfred H. Terry
and party to the Canadian boundary, where Terry was to cross over,
meet Sitting Bull, and attempt to induce him to return to the United
States. Two days previous, Company K, Seventh Cavalry, under Captain
Owen Hale, set out on the same mission, only to be recalled (and subsequently overtaken by the Second Cavalry companies) on orders from
departmental headquarters. Field Return, Battalion Second Cavalry,
September, 1877. NAMP M744, Roll 166; Major George Gibson to
AAGDD, October 1, 1877, in *Report of the Secretary of War, 1877*, 546–47.
    18. Miles did not learn of the Nez Perce situation until the evening
of September 17 (see footnote 20). Zimmer, of course, could not have
known of Miles's plans at this date, further suggesting that the journal
contents expanded upon a much briefer diary entry.

might have been but we had no place to carry the carcasses. This evening we have no water for our stock & but little for ourselves & fuel the same as last night.

" *20th.*

Weather cool. We left camp early in search of water. We are, & have been, on K Co. 7th trail who started for Fort Benton[19] 2 days ahead of us. At 9 A.M. we came to a creek of alkali water and here found K Co. 7th Cav. in camp. A courier had overtaken them with orders for to stop until we caught up. We stayed here until 2 P.M., then moved up a few miles further & went in camp on the same stream. No wood, & buffalo chips had to be used instead. The country has not been rough, but very poor & in places entirely barren. Buffalo & antelope were not as plenty. Buffalo meat is not as good as I thought it would be. It tastes much like poor beef. Perhaps a yearling calf would be good. Those we

---

19. Fort Benton stood on the left bank of the Missouri River, at the head of steam navigation of that stream. Erected in 1847 by Pierre Chouteau and Company, in 1850 it was formally named for Senator Thomas Hart Benton (1782–1858) of Missouri. The Northwest Fur Company purchased the post in 1866 and three years later leased the facility to the army. Troops garrisoned the old fur company buildings until 1874, when more suitable quarters were acquired in the adjoining community of Fort Benton. From its position at the head of navigation, the post received supplies for distribution to interior stations, such as Fort Shaw, north of Helena, and Fort Ellis, far to the south. Freight and trade goods from Fort Benton also traveled overland to North-West Mounted Police stations in Canada. The one-company post also served as eastern terminus of the Mullan Road from Fort Walla Walla, Washington Territory. Miller and Cohen, *Military and Trading Posts of Montana*, 12–14; William E. Lass, "The History and Significance of the Northwest Fur Company, 1865–1869," *North Dakota History: Journal of the Northern Plains*, 61 (Summer 1994), 40; Joel Overholser, *Fort Benton: World's Innermost Port* (Fort Benton, Mont.: privately published, 1987).

had were from 2 to 4 years old. Antelope & deer are very good eating, much better than good mutton.

September 21st.
Weather cloudy & cold, & tonight it's commencing to rain. The country has been better than yesterday but the grass is cropped close to the ground. Antelope are plenty & buffalo are here, I should judge, by the hundreds of thousands. About 40 of the former were killed between all the Co. This afternoon Gen. Miles overtook us with Co. A & D of the 7th Cavalry & 4 cos. of his infantry, mounted. They were traveling with packs [mules]. The wagon train is coming in the rear with one co. of infantry as guard.[20] We have wood tonight, but the water is worse than last night.

" 22nd.
Weather & country the same as yesterday. Buffalo & antelope are more plenty than yesterday, but no shooting was allowed for fear of stampeding them and putting the Indians on their guard, if there is any near. Gen. Miles brought 20 Cheyenne Indians with him who are sent to the right & left flank every day to scout.[21] Wood is plenty, but water is scarce & bad.

---

20. Miles had departed the Yellowstone on September 18, after having received on the previous evening a dispatch from General Howard announcing that the Nez Perces had eluded both him and Colonel Samuel D. Sturgis and were heading due north, possibly to join forces with Sitting Bull in Canada. Gibson to AAGDD, October 1, 1877, in *Report of the Secretary of War, 1877*, 547. This movement changed the mission of the Second Cavalry units, previously directed to serve as escort to General Terry's commission to Sitting Bull, and now absorbed, along with Company K, Seventh Cavalry, into Miles's campaign against the Nez Perces.

21. The Northern Cheyennes had surrendered to Miles at the Tongue River Cantonment in March, and at least thirty of them subsequently signed on as scouts for his command. Greene, *Yellowstone Command*, 198.

" *23rd.*

Weather quite fair. The country has been quite rough this forenoon. This afternoon it's been more than rough. We reached Squaw Creek and traveled down it until we reached its mouth, where it empties into the Missouri River 6 miles below the Musselshell River. Several wagons were upset & poles broken and it was 9 P.M. before we went in camp on the banks of the Missouri River. (A courier was sent ahead this morning to stop any steamer that was either going up or down, & he just happened to strike one going down from Ft. Benton loaded with robes & furs.) The river here is well timbered. The steamer is unloading tonight and getting ready to take us over in the morning.

September 24th.

Weather fair. We crossed the river on the steamer *Fontenelle*[22] & it was night before everything of ours was over. We are camped on a very nice bottom with good grass and lots of wood. The bottom is not wide & in the rear there is a range of bad looking hills. General Miles & command will cross tomorrow.

" *25th.*

Weather fair. Gen. Miles has been crossing his command all day, & at 5 P.M. none of his large train had been touched. We remained in camp until 6 P.M., when we moved up on

---

22. The *Fontenelle* was a wood-hulled sternwheel packet built in 1870. Measuring 205 feet long by 34 wide, the vessel spent much time on the upper Missouri, with numerous trips to Fort Benton, Cow Island, and Carroll. The *Fontenelle* had been frozen in the river above Fort Sully, Dakota Territory, for much of the winter of 1876–77. It was finally cut down by ice and destroyed in 1881. *Way's Packet Directory*, 169.

the hill 2 miles so as to get a early start in the morning. One of Miles's scouts by the name of Johnson[23] got drowned in the Missouri yesterday while trying to swim it with his horse. A small boat with 2 men in it came down the river at dark. They report Nez Perces crossing the river at Cow Island. This is head of low water navigation and the government had some warehouses here & when necessary freighting was done with mule & ox trains to Ft. Benton. The Nez Perces Indians after crossing destroyed all the government stores what they did not take along, and an ox train that was coming to load up.[24] Cow Island is 150 miles above us. The Indians are on their way to the British Possessions.

September 26th.

We had a heavy wind storm during the night and the day has been windy & cold. They have been working all night in crossing the train & it's not over yet. We were on our way by 4 A.M. up the river. After the first 4 hours the country has been a high prairie poorly watered. But buffalo &

---

23. The man who perished was George Johnson, who had served Miles as a scout since the late summer of 1876. Greene, *Yellowstone Command*, 257n.

24. The Nez Perces destroyed approximately fifty tons of government and commercial supplies at Cow Island Landing, making repeated attacks on the small garrison of twelve Seventh infantrymen and four civilians during the night of September 23. Two of the civilians were wounded in the fight, which lasted until after dawn of the 24th. The next day, the Indians attacked a wagon train headed north, then engaged a small command of volunteers from Fort Benton, forcing its withdrawal back to the Missouri. The tribesmen continued traveling north. *Record of Engagements with Hostile Indians within the Military Division of the Missouri, from 1868 to 1882, Lieutenant-General P. H. Sheridan, Commanding* (Washington, D.C.: Government Printing Office, 1882), 73; Brown, *Flight of the Nez Perce*, 369–77.

antelope til one can't rest. 4 of the former were killed. Our camp is on a bright clear stream & wood enough, but the grass has been cropped very short.

" *27th.*
Weather quite pleasant. Just as we were about to move out of camp this morning, Gen. Miles & command, except the train, put in their appearance & put a stop to our movement. About noon their train hove in sight & by 4 P.M. each co. had 8 days' rations on pack mules & we were soon on our way again. The Indians did not stop at all but kept ahead. We traveled until 11 P.M. in the darkness through a country much the same as the fore part of the evening. Here we went in camp near a hole in the ground with some stinking water but no wood.

September 28th.
Weather windy. We were up by 3 A.M. gathering buffalo chips to cook breakfast with & by 5 were on our way. We found some good water 2 miles ahead. Here we watered our horses (the water [at camp] this morning was so bad that they would not drink it) & filled our canteens. The country is a rolling prairie, but to our left & ahead there is a range of rough-looking hills called Little Rocky. When we got close to the foot of them we saw a herd of bear some 20 in number, but from where we were up to where they were was some 2 miles & very steep at that. If it had of been a good road I think the officers would have let some of the ambitious overtake them. This evening we are camped on a bright stream running from these hills (in the East they would be fearful big mountains) where wood & grass is plenty.

" *29th.*

Weather rainy & cold. The country for the first few hours were the same as yesterday. Then they changed to hilly & rocky. We went in camp at 3 P.M. on account of the weather near a pond of water. Wood very scarce & buffalo chips had to be used along with what we got. After we got in camp it began to snow & by night several inches had fallen. (The worst of it was we had no tents. They were in the wagons which were left back with Miles's train. During the summer we carried small tents on our horses, but after we came off of the Little Missouri River trip we turned them in and drew the A tent, which has to be carried in wagons or on pack mules, & of them there wasn't enough allowed to a co. to bring them.)

September 30th.

Weather thawing. There's not as much snow now as there was on going to bed last night. The cooks had great trouble in getting us something warm for breakfast this morning, wood being gone & the chips we gathered last night are so wet it's lots of work a-fanning to get them to burn. Yet by 6 we had our wet dunnage packed & on the way. 2 half-breeds & 3 or 4 Indians went on yesterday afternoon to strike the Nez Perces' trail if they had come over so far. We had marched about 2½ hours when we saw the scouts coming back full tilt. The command halted & we learned that the Nez Perces' camp was about 5 miles ahead (this is about 60 miles from the British Possessions).[25] Extra clothing were stripped & every man supplied himself with 100 rounds of ammunition. Cheyenne Indians were making themselves ready at the same time by doing away with their blankets &

---

25. The distance is actually about forty miles.

adorning themselves & ponies with feathers & their war hats. In a short time everything was in readiness & we started off at a brisk trot, leaving one co. of infantry with the pack train. A messenger was sent at once back to the train to have the 12 pounder & some shell brought up at once. (I forgot to mention that we had a small rifle cannon like the one we [also] had on the Little Missouri River trip along.)

We soon got sight of their camp, which was down in a ravine on both sides of a small stream called Snake Creek. The 3 cos. of the 7th Cavalry got orders to charge the camp, while our 3 cos. were to make for the pony herd [on] the other side of their camp, while the infantry were to come up in the rear. The 7th tried to get in their camp, but it was no go. The banks were too steep & in their turning around to try another place the Indians, who were lying under the bank, rose up and gave them a volley which killed & wounded many. They then dismounted along with the infantry & [the] little cannon gave them Hell. About this time 40 Indians mounted their ponies & surrounded a small group of ponies & took for the high ground. G Co. of our battalion were sent after them & recaptured the ponies, but the Indians made good their escape. H Co. went to the assistance of the 7th & infantry, while our co. were engaged in gathering up the loose ponies that were scattered about the prairie. After this was done, they were drove down in a ravine and a guard put around them (of which there was about 1200 ponies) & the rest of us went in the skirmish line. Firing was kept up until after dark. The Indians had a good natural fortified camp. They done but little shooting & it was only once in a while that one showed himself. After dark our skirmish line was brought around so as to completely hem them in to prevent their escape. Once in a while our men would fire a volley at their camp so as to let them know that we were about, & if possible to prevent their further fortifying. Our number killed & wounded is supposed to be about 30, & [these] were left lying, except those that were able to crawl in our lines & that was few. Our co. had 2 wounded, one in the right elbow & the other in the hip. We remain in the line all night.[26]

October 1st.

The night was quite cold & during the day it's either been snowing or raining. About daylight the Indians put up a white rag as a signal for surrender. This gave us a chance to get our dead & wounded. Quite a number had died during the night from exposure, & one man was found with his throat cut. He was shot through the bowels. It's supposed that he did it with his own hands. The sight is frightful to see so many dead soldiers, Indians, horses & ponies lying about. Lieut. Jerome[27] of H Co. was sent in the Indian camp

---

26. The Battle of the Bear's Paw Mountains was the climactic engagement of the Nez Perce War. It occurred in what is now Blaine County, Montana, approximately fifteen miles south of the present community of Chinook. The standoff between Miles and the Nez Perces lasted from September 30 until October 5. The initial day's fighting brought the heaviest casualties for the troops, with two officers and sixteen men killed and four officers and forty-four men (including two Indian scouts) wounded—all in the space of a few hours. Subsequently, the engagement assumed the character of a siege, with Miles's soldiers surrounding the Indian village until the tribesmen yielded. While some of the Indians finally escaped to Canada, 418—mostly women and children—surrendered to Miles on the battlefield. *Record of Engagements*, 73–74. For further particulars of the Bear's Paw action, see Brown, *Flight of the Nez Perce*, 388–409; and McWhorter, *Hear Me, My Chiefs!* 478–507.

27. Lovell H. Jerome (1849–1935), born to a prominent New York City family, upon graduation from the Military Academy in 1870 was appointed to the Second Cavalry. He served at Fort Ellis, Montana

& Chief Joseph[28] came in ours to hold a confab with Gen. Miles. He, Joseph, wanted his ponies back & to be left alone. This Gen. Miles would not agree to, but told him they must surrender unconditional. So Chief Joseph went back to his camp to hold council with his other chiefs & warriors, [we] thinking of course that they would let Lieut. Jerome come out. But night came & [he] was still there. They thought that we would not fire on them as long as they kept him in there and they could fortify themselves better, which they did. Just before dark the interpreter was sent in their camp & told Jerome to get in as safe a place as

---

Territory, for most of his military career and had participated in the Lame Deer Fight in May 1877. Jerome was a highly regarded officer, but a chronic drinking problem forced him to resign his commission in April 1879. He later enlisted in the army, but was discharged a corporal in 1882. In civil life, Jerome managed a Tennessee mining company, attempted mining in Alaska, and took a job with the U.S. Customs Service. He died in New York City. Carroll and Price, *Roll Call on the Little Big Horn*, 68; Harold G. Stearns, "The Volunteer Hostage," *Montana The Magazine of Western History*, 18 (October 1968), 87–89.

28. Joseph (1840–1904), whose Nez Perce name was Heinmot Tooyalakekt, which translated to "Thunder traveling to loftier mountain heights," was leader of the Wallowa band of Nez Perces, one of the groups that had joined in arms against the maltreatment by whites and the U.S. government that had precipitated the conflict. Born in 1840, he was the son of Wellamotkin, known to whites as "Old Joseph." After the death of Old Joseph in 1871, Young Joseph emerged as a major spokesman on behalf of his people, participating in councils with government representatives, but never affiliating with those tribal leaders who accepted prescribed reservation boundaries. Joseph and others of the so-called "nontreaty" Nez Perce leaders led their people 1,700 miles in their effort to evade the soldiers and reach Canada. After the surrender at Bear's Paw, Joseph—the only remaining principal leader, the others having escaped or been killed—accompanied the surviving Nez Perces to Indian Territory (Oklahoma), where they stayed until 1885. Joseph died on the Colville Reservation in Washington. Alvin M. Josephy, *The Patriot Chiefs: A Chronicle of American Indian Resistance* (New York: The Viking Press, 1958), 313–40.

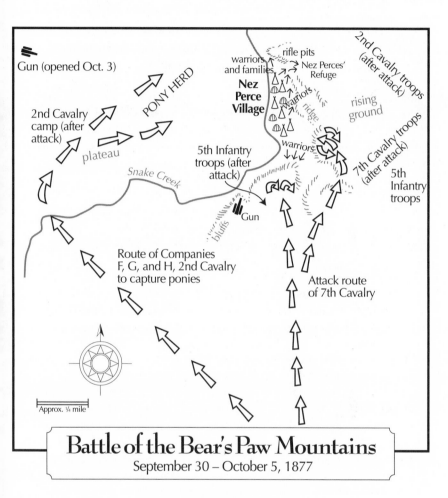

Gun (opened Oct. 3)

2nd Cavalry camp (after attack)

PONY HERD

plateau

Snake Creek

Route of Companies F, G, and H, 2nd Cavalry to capture ponies

Approx. ¼ mile

warriors and families

rifle pits

Nez Perces' Refuge

Nez Perce Village

warriors

ridge

rising ground

2nd Cavalry troops (after attack)

7th Cavalry troops (after attack)

5th Infantry troops

5th Infantry troops (after attack)

warriors

Gun

bluffs

Attack route of 7th Cavalry

Battle of the Bear's Paw Mountains
September 30 – October 5, 1877

MAP BY JEROME A. GREENE AND KATHRYN FEHLIG

possible, that firing would commence at once to prevent their working.[29] Our whole train arrived just before dark, also the big gun. During the day 24 of our men were buried & 32 wounded are now lying in the hospital tents. This includes all our killed, 2 officers of K Co. 7th Cav. & 2 Cheyenne Indians.[30] Firing is to be kept up from time to time during the night. All hands are to be out again.

October 2nd.

Last night was a fearful one. It blew very hard & about 3 inches of snow fell. It snowed some during the day & it's been very cold. Several of our wounded died during the night & 2 more of our men were killed during the firing about morning. One of G Co., our battalion. The other was from the 5th Infantry. Our battalion got relieved off of the skirmish line this evening. No firing has been going on since daylight. The Indians have split. Chief Joseph wants to surrender & White Bird[31] wants to fight it out. Lieut. Jerome

---

29. Zimmer is mistaken regarding the detention of Lieutenant Jerome. In fact, Miles decided to detain Joseph overnight, and the Indians in turn held Lieutenant Jerome. The prisoners were exchanged on the morning of October 2.

30. See part 2, footnote 26, above for precise casualty figures. No Indian scouts were killed.

31. White Bird (ca. 1807–1892) was leader of the Lamtamas band of Nez Perces, representing a major portion of the coalition of disaffected tribesmen that fought the army. A brave hunter in his youth, White Bird proved intractable toward government negotiators who would reduce the Nez Perce land base. In councils he was noted for betraying little emotion, often covering his face from view with an eagle's wing. At Bear's Paw, on the night of October 5, White Bird and some 130 followers penetrated the encircling soldiers and escaped to Canada, where the Teton Sioux leader, Sitting Bull, welcomed them. White Bird later rebuffed emmissaries from Miles seeking his surrender. He remained in Canada for the rest of his life. Brown, *Flight of the Nez Perce*,

was released this morning. He reports that their strength is 250 besides a large number of squaws & children, also that Chief Looking Glass & Chief Joseph's brother[32] are amongst the killed. The Indians have been working faithful all day, & we've not been idle. Those on duty have been throwing up breastworks & putting the two cannons in good positions behind good works. We will see what tomorrow will bring forth. Our strength is about 325 enlisted men.

October 3rd.
The weather has been disagreeable most of the day. It's snowing off & on until dark. Firing has been going on all day & their camp got a good shelling. But they are well fixed & intend to wear us out. Their rifle pits have underground connections, & if a shot strikes in one they crawl through to another. Our battalion was supporting the big guns on the north side of their camp.

" *4th.*
Weather some warmer. Our battalion has been doing various duty. Some have been sent after wood, which is in the hills 5 miles distance, & others have been herding the captured ponies, while some were in rifle pits popping at the Indians whenever one made his appearance.

82–83; McWhorter, *Hear Me, My Chiefs!* 181–82; John D. McDermott, *Forlorn Hope: The Battle of White Bird Canyon and the Beginning of the Nez Perce War* (Boise: Idaho State Historical Society, 1978), 34, 162.

32. Looking Glass (ca. 1830s–1877) was leader of the Alpowais band of Nez Perces. A widely respected warrior and chief, he counseled peace with the troops until they attacked his village on July 1, 1877, whereupon he joined forces with White Bird, Joseph, and their followers. Joseph's younger brother was Ollokot, a noted warrior chief of the Wallowa band. McWhorter, *Hear Me, My Chiefs!* 178, 182.

" *5th.*

It froze very hard last night, but the sun came out bright & warm this morning. Last night our men crawled up on the Indians works, within 50 yards, & dug pits under the shelter of the darkness & a heavy fire from our men. As soon as it was dawn our boys began to poor lead into their pits and by ten A.M. they squealed. White rags could be seen in all directions in their camp. Our officers met their chiefs half way & had a talk & soon after Joseph's people brought in their arms & ammunition. White Bird & Looking Glass's people want to hear from their people in the hills first before they surrender, so a few were let go to hold council with them, but leaving their arms. Our duty was the same as yesterday. The wood party brought in several buffalo this evening.

October 6th.

Weather quite warm. This fight is over. Last night Chief White Bird crawled through our lines with a few followers & made their escape. The remainder of his & Looking Glass's people came out & gave up their arms & the work of moving them out of their old camp was soon begun.[33] Our men were put in their camp to overhaul their works. They found quite a number of Indians buried, also some rifles & ammunition. One Indian was found buried alive with his hip broke. He had a rifle, ammunition & several days provisions, with various other articles of plunder. (It's likely he expected some of his escaped friends would come for him. He was in a tunnel dividing two pits, with each end of the tunnel banked up nearly to the top.) Our guard duty will be much lighter this evening.

---

33. Looking Glass was himself killed at Bear's Paw.

October 7th.

Weather windy & threatening. The Indian pony herd has been on the increase ever since we came. Its number is now about 1500. They were scattered about the prairie for miles around. White Bird has not been heard of since his escape. Since the surrender the Indians say it was wholly his fault in their standing out as long as they did. Gen. Miles started for Tongue River Post at 10 A.M. His infantry & the 3 cos. of the 7th cav. are to take the Indians & ponies along. The wounded & the two dead officers are to be taken to the Missouri River & shipped on the first boat that happens to pass. The number of dead Indians is 43 & the number of wounded so far as they have asked for [medical] attendance is 67. Our killed is 26, wounded 42 (I think some of our wounded have died since).[34] Those Indians that lit out as soon as the fight commenced went for reinforcements. They started for the British line & on their way on Milk River found a camp of Gros Ventre & Assiniboin Indians. Instead of them helping, they killed 14 Nez Perces & took quite a number of their ponies. So two Canadian Frenchmen tell us this evening, they having been told by the balance of the Nez Perces that got away. It's only 60 [actually 40] miles to the line & only a few miles further to the trading post where these men

---

34. Total casualties at Bear's Paw Mountains for Miles's command numbered twenty-one killed and fifty-two wounded, including two Indian scouts. The Nez Perces lost about twenty-five killed and perhaps forty-five wounded. Dr. Henry M. Tilton to Medical Director, Department of Dakota, October 3, 1877, Entry 624, Box 1, RG 94, NA; McWhorter, *Hear Me, My Chiefs!* 486. See also, Miles to AAGDD, October 6, 1877, in *Report of the Secretary of War, 1877*, 515–16. Several of the wounded died en route to the Tongue River Cantonment.

belong. Our battalion is to stay here until tomorrow some time when we are to start for Ft. Ellis via Ft. Benton.[35]

October 8th.

It rained all last night & up to noon today. Before we left camp a white scout & 7 Cheyenne Indians from Gen. Miles's command passed us. They are going to try & find Chief White Bird. We went in camp early for the sake of getting both wood & water. The country has been a nice prairie all day, with Bear Paw Mountain just ahead.

October 9th.

Weather very fine, & the country up to noon the same as yesterday. At that time we reached Milk River, also the mixed camp of 80 lodges of Indians (spoken of here before).[36] This place is called Belknap.[37] It used to be the agency for various tribes of Indians. The stockade & log warehouses are standing yet & occupied by a trader. These Indians now have to go to the Missouri River for their

---

35. The Second Cavalry battalion was directed to resume its march to Fort Benton to escort the Sitting Bull Commission to the Canadian border, from which assignment it had been diverted to assist in the prosecution of the Nez Perces. Field Return, Second Cavalry Battalion, October, 1877, NAMP M744, Roll 166.

36. The camp of Assiniboins and Gros Ventres is mentioned in the entry for October 7.

37. Established in 1871 as a trading post, Fort Belknap, named for then-Secretary of War William Worth Belknap, stood on the south side of Milk River. In 1873 it became the first permanent agency for the Gros Ventre (Atsina) Indians, but in 1876 it closed temporarily because of insufficient congressional funding. Reopened two years later, Fort Belknap functioned at its original site until 1888, when it was relocated near Harlem, Montana Territory. Miller and Cohen, *Military and Trading Posts of Montana*, 11.

yearly allowance from the government. We went up the river a few miles further & went in camp. The river bottom is very rich & grass is good. This river is about 30 yards wide & shallow, yet it's bad crossing on account of quicksand. It's not very well wooded, only in places. It has a milky color owing to the soil it runs through. Here where we are camped are the ruins of a large ranch or trading place. The guide tells us that the soldiers destroyed it 2 years ago on account of the owners' trading ammunition to the Sioux Indians.[38]

October 10th.
Weather fair. We soon left the river & the country is not as good. It's more like that of the 8th only better watered. About 2 P.M. we met E Co. of the 7th Cavalry from Ft. Benton on their way to Fort Lincoln for winter quarters. Our rations being nearly out, & they having more than they needed, they let us have some, also oats for our horses.

" 11th.
Weather fine, & so was the country all day & well watered with beautiful clear streams. These streams take their rise in the Little Rocky & Bear Paw region. On the one that we are camped tonight, & just a few rods above us, there is a Gros Ventre camp of 40 or 50 lodges. All of these streams

---

38. In 1875 troops from Forts Shaw and Ellis worked to suppress illegal whiskey traffic in the Upper Missouri country. *Report of the Secretary of War, 1875* (Washington, D.C.: Government Printing Office, 1875), 62–65. The destroyed establishment was likely Power's Post, situated at the confluence of the Milk and Big Sandy rivers and operated by the T. C. Power Company. Miller and Cohen, *Military and Trading Posts of Montana*, 73.

are yet alive with beaver, otter & muskrats. Brush wood is generally plenty.

" *12th.*

Weather & country the same as yesterday except water. We had to make a very long march in order to get some, & that we did get is scarcely fit to drink, & there is no wood, so we were obliged to use buffalo chips. Here we found in camp General Terry[39] with 5 peace commissioners[40] & one holy

---

39. Brigadier General Alfred H. Terry (1827–1890), who led the Sitting Bull Commission into Canada, was commander of the Military Department of Dakota, with headquarters at Fort Snelling, St. Paul, Minnesota. A Yale-educated lawyer, Terry was colonel of the Second Connecticut Volunteer Infantry, and later of the Seventh Connecticut Volunteer Infantry, serving in the early Civil War campaigns in northern Virginia and participating in the movement into South Carolina and Georgia. As brigadier general of volunteers, Terry played a role in numerous engagements, including that at Fort Pulaski, Georgia, and in the operations against Forts Sumter and Wagner, South Carolina. In Virginia again, he commanded the division of the X Corps in the actions around Richmond and Petersburg, Virginia, and as major general of volunteers commanded the expedition that captured Fort Fisher, North Carolina, for which he received the thanks of Congress and a brevet of major general. Promoted brigadier general in the regular army in 1865, Terry assumed command of the Department of Dakota in September 1866. He commanded the eastern wing of the campaign against the Teton Sioux in 1876, playing a role in the controversy surrounding the Little Bighorn disaster. Terry retired as major general in 1888. Carroll and Price, *Roll Call on the Little Big Horn*, 158–59; Heitman, *Historical Register and Dictionary*, 1:951; *Records of Living Officers of the United States Army*, 8.

40. Besides Terry, the other commissioner was diplomat Albert G. Lawrence, of Rhode Island. They were accompanied by Captain Henry C. Corbin, Twenty-fourth Infantry, secretary; Mr. Jay Stone, of St. Paul, stenographer; and Baptiste Shane, interpreter. *Report of the Commission Appointed by Direction of the President of the United States . . . to Meet the Sioux Indian Chief, Sitting Bull* (Washington, D.C.: Government Printing Office, 1877), 4–6.

Jo [priest] & a few infantry of the 7th belonging to Fort Shaw. They were on their way to the British Possessions to hold a confab with Sitting Bull & other chiefs of the Sioux tribes, & it's reported that we are to turn back & accompany him. Just before going in camp we saw a very large flock of antelope, the first game we saw since leaving the battlefield.

October 13th.

It froze very hard last night, yet the weather has been very pleasant today. We took our back trail for 5 miles, then took to the north. Water has been very scarce all day, & where we are camped there is none. We brought a little along to make coffee & the chips had to be used instead of wood. Buffalo were here during the summer by the thousand when water was plenty, so our guide tells us, but in the fall of the year, when these basins become dry, they shoulder their hump and make for parts where living streams are more plenty. (The hump of a buffalo is the tenderest part about one. This is a chunk of flesh on the top of the neck weighing from 10 to 20 pounds, according to the size of the beast, & when they gallop they draw in their necks. [This] brings the hump on their shoulders, which makes them look at a distance like an elephant.)

" *14th.*

Weather pleasant. Last night a courier came in from the British line saying that the chief will wait but a few days longer, that they have been waiting at Fort Walsh for a week & that they are anxious to go back to their tribes (which are at the present near Cypress Mountains the other side of

Fort Walsh.[41] Fort Walsh is the nearest British military post to the U.S. frontier lines). So this morning the best teams were loaded light and H Co. & 12 men of the infantry (who were put in wagons) started off with the commission & two reporters, one of the Chicago & one for the New York Times.[42] The other 2 cos. & the balance of the train are to move on as usual. This evening we are camped on Milk River again, only further up, & 2 of the wagons are stuck in the quicksand & they are likely to stay there until morning.

October 15th.

Weather fair, and the country all it lacks is wood & water to make it a splendid one. We had some trouble in getting the wagons out, but once out they rolled right along. The trail was perfectly level. Tonight we are camped on a pool of water that the last snow left. No wood, so we had to use its substitute.

---

41. Fort Walsh was one of several North-West Mounted Police outposts established initially to help stem among the Canadian natives the American whiskey trade emanating from Fort Benton, Montana. Built in 1875 by Inspector James Walsh, for whom it was named, Fort Walsh stood in a pine-studded valley of the otherwise barren Cypress Hills, a log stockade surrounding its principal buildings. The police post played a key role in control of the various tribes entering Canada from the United States during the turbulent late 1870s. Fort Walsh was abandoned in 1882 and demolished the following year. John Peter Turner, *The North-West Mounted Police, 1873–1893*, 2 vols. (Ottawa: Edmond Cloutier, 1950), 1:212–15, 323, 661; 2:8; Robert M. Utley, *Lance and the Shield*, 184; R. G. MacBeth, *Policing the Plains: Being the Real-Life Record of the Famous Royal North-West Mounted Police* (Philadelphia: David McKay Company, 1931), 34, 62–63.

42. Charles Sanford Diehl, representing the *Chicago Times*, and Jerome B. Stillson representing the *New York Herald*, accompanied the commission. Oliver N. Knight, *Following the Indian Wars: The Story of the Newspaper Correspondents among the Indian Campaigners* (Norman: University of Oklahoma Press, 1960), 296.

" *16th.*

Weather & country the same as yesterday. About 1 P.M. we reached a sheet of water called Wild Horse Lake. Here Co. H lay in camp. They got here yesterday at 1 P.M. They went to the line with Gen. Terry & party, then returned to where we found them. The line is only 1½ mile from here. There Terry was met by an expected escort of 50 British cavalry & Gen. Walsh[43] (the British cavalry on the frontier are called mounted police). Twelve infantrymen went along with Terry & party and they were disarmed before crossing to the British soil. Fort Walsh is 30 miles from the line. We are to remain here with H Co. until Terry returns. This Lake, I am told, is from 50 to 60 miles long & from 1 to 5 miles wide. The most of it is across the line. It has no outlet or inlet that is constant. It is supplied by the rain & snow that falls on the surrounding prairie, which is very flat. We can ride our horses in it for half a mile & not get our boots wet. There's no fish in it, at least in this part where we are, & not a sprig of wood is to be seen on its banks. But water fowl are plenty & of all kind, from the swan down to the common lake or river gull. As there is no wood here, each co. took a wagon & went to gathering substitutes, enough to

---

43. Inspector James Morrow Walsh (1840–1905) had joined the North-West Mounted Police on its organization in 1873 and had been in charge in the Cypress Hills since 1875, erecting there the police post of Fort Walsh. He became the dominant personality with whom U.S. government, as well as Sioux, leaders were forced to deal during the turbulent period following the Lakota hegira to Canada. In later years Walsh engaged in the coal business and eventually became civil governor of the Yukon Territory. MacBeth, *Policing the Plains*, 34–35, 62; William R. Morrison, *Showing the Flag: The Mounted Police and Canadian Sovereignty, 1894–1925* (Vancouver: University of British Columbia Press, 1985), 191n.

last us during our stay here. Buffalo must have been very plenty here & that not long since. One of our men shot a badger this evening. This is the first one I ever saw. Their burrows are very plenty out here. As there is none in the East, I will try to describe it. In shape, they are very much like the ground mole, long nose, short legs & stumpy tail. They are from 2½ to 3 feet in length & very heavy. They are spotted gray & white & their hair are like the woodchucks. Their ears are short & pointed & from between the ears down to the tip of the nose there is a snow white stripe.

October 17th.
Weather fair. Deer & antelope come down to the lake by the 100 in the morning to drink so it's no trouble for us to get what kind suits us best. I like antelope best. Grass is gnawed down very close for several miles about the lake.

" *18th.*
Weather remains fair. A courier came from Gen. Terry this evening. Says Terry & party will reach us tomorrow at 12 M & for us to be ready to start back. Says that the chiefs don't want to have anything to do with the United States, and from this [time] out they are a-going to live with the queen.

" *19th.*
Weather fair. Gen. Terry hove in sight at the appointed time & we were ready to start back with him. This evening we are camped at the mud hole where we were the 15th.

" *20th.*

Weather fair. Game of all kind very plenty. Got one buffalo. (On the 15th when we came along here there wasn't a living thing in sight.) Tonight we are again camped on Milk River.

" *21st.*

Weather fair. The list of game increases some today. Two skunks are amongst the seen. We made a big day's march, that is, and have teams along. This evening we are camped on a little swamp. Ducks are very plenty and so is rotten water. There is a small ox train stopping here for the night. It's on the way to Fort Walsh from Ft. Benton. Nearly all the supplies for this post is brought through the United States.

October 22nd.

Weather beautiful. We left camp very early & by 3 P.M. came to the camp where we met Terry. Just before dark we crossed the Marias River where the Teton River empties into the latter. The last 10 miles were very rolling & full of ravines. The rivers are both nice sparkling streams from 3 to 6 rods wide. Their valleys are very narrow & [contain] poor soil. We are camped a short distance from the mouth of the Teton on its banks. Here there is an Indian trader & at present about a dozen lodges around him of different tribes. (Several miles up the Marias River from where we crossed it, Major Baker with our battalion destroyed a whole camp of Piegan Indians in the winter of 1870 & 71. He marched all night, starting from Ft. Benton, & reached their camp just at daybreak. The snow

was from 18 inches to 2 feet deep, and but 2 Indians escaped with their lives. They had been thieving & murder-
ing the miners & settlers about Deer Lodge, Montana. I
was told this by men of our co. who were there & no
doubt but it's the truth.)[44]

" *23rd.*

Weather beautiful. We left camp late & after crossing &
recrossing the Teton River a dozen times we left it, turning
to our left, & by 11 A.M. reached Ft. Benton and the mighty
Missouri River, although it's not very mighty here & especially at this time of the year. It still keeps a good width, but
it's so shallow that the smallest steamer can't get up. Fort
Benton is surrounded by a town of the same name, population 800. The Northwestern Fur Co. has its agents here.
They came here when the fort was first built years ago &
they have some very large storehouses.[45] There is but one

---

44. On January 23, 1870, Major Eugene M. Baker led four companies
of the Second Cavalry (the "Montana Battalion") and a detachment of
mounted infantry in an assault on a large body of Piegan Indians camped
along the Marias and wrongly thought to be another village allegedly
responsible for recent attacks on settlers. One hundred seventy-three tribesmen died in the dawn assault, including many women and children. Many
noncombatants were also captured. The assault precipitated a major controversy over the military's role in the evolving "Peace Policy," the plan to
end the difficulties with the Indians through oversight by a board of phi-
lanthropists and religious entities. Major Baker was vilified in the eastern
press for leading the "Massacre on the Marias" in which but one soldier
was killed. *Record of Engagements with Hostile Indians*, 26; Paul A. Hutton,
Phil Sheridan and His Army (Lincoln: University of Nebraska Press, 1985),
188–200; Utley, *Frontier Regulars*, 190–91. A book-length account sympa-
thetic to Baker is Robert J. Ege, *Tell Baker to Strike Them Hard: Incident on the
Marias* (Bellevue, Neb.: Old Army Press, 1970).

45. Following problems resulting from conflicting schemes and
personal animosities, the Northwest Fur Company's partners signed a

co. of infantry in the fort.[46] We are to remain here until tomorrow morning.

October 24th.

This morning opened fine, but it soon became windy & tonight it's raining. We made 28 miles. Our course was up the river a few miles, then we left it to our left. The country has been a nice rolling prairie. Where we are camped there is a ranch. Wood was bought, water is plenty but poor. Last night at Benton two men of H Co., while under the influence of liquor, got in a quarrel & one shot the other not seriously.

" *25th.*

Weather windy & cold. The country is more hilly than yesterday & water more plenty. Cattle are scattered all over the country, yet we saw no more ranches until we reached Sun River, where we are camped. This is a clear & swift running stream, not deep or wide. Wood is plenty in places. This stream has a very wide bottom & very rich ranches are seen in numbers. There is a semi-weekly stage [that] runs over this trail from Benton to Ft. Shaw.

---

dissolution accord in 1869, ending their involvement in the fur-trading business although agreeing to maintain a scaled-back operation at Fort Benton to help settle accounts. The army continued to rent the post from the former partners, who maintained an agent at Fort Benton for several years to oversee their holdings. In 1874, the troops removed to leased buildings in the adjacent town of the same name. Lass, "History and Significance of the Northwest Fur Company," 24, 30–31, 38, 40; Frazer, *Forts of the West*, 79.

46. The twenty-nine men of Company F, Seventh Infantry, occupied Fort Benton. *Report of the Secretary of War, 1877,* 37.

October 26th.

Weather cold & windy. We made an early start & by noon reached Ft. Shaw.[47] This is a nice fort. The buildings are either stone or adobe brick. It's on a high piece of ground & close to Sun Riv. In the rear there is some high hills, and over them about 30 miles distance one can see the snow-covered Rocky Mountains. The trail followed the river all the way from our last night camp to Fort Shaw. It's well settled, some farming is done, but the principal business is cattle & they may be seen roaming about in herds of thousands. (I said Sun River was well settled. Yes, it's very thickly settled. I don't think any one man owned more than 80 or 100 rods front on the river, & at this width they own back to the hills or high prairie land, which is at present government land & everyone lets his cattle run.) Fort Shaw was built for a 6-co. post, but at present there is only 3 cos. of the 7th Infantry in it. It was built in 1867 & since then all these settlers have moved in on the river bottom.

" *27th.*

Weather cold but not windy. The trail, or rather toll road, which it is, ran through a very rocky & hilly country, yet

---

47. Fort Shaw, located on the right bank of Sun River, was established in 1867 to guard the route between Fort Benton, to the northeast, and Helena, to the south, as well as to prevent incursions by Indians against settlements in the region. In 1876–77 Fort Shaw was home to the Seventh Infantry and was headquarters of the Military District of Montana under Colonel John Gibbon. Troops from Fort Shaw took part in numerous campaigns against Blackfeet and Teton Sioux tribesmen. Named for Colonel Robert Gould Shaw, who had headed the all-black Fifty-fourth Massachusetts Volunteer Infantry during the Civil War, the post was abandoned in 1891. Thereafter, until 1910, the buildings functioned as an Indian school. Frazer, *Forts of the West*, 83–84; Miller and Cohen, *Military and Trading Posts of Montana*, 76–80.

we passed quite a number of ranches. One was a sheep ranch. We saw one flock & two men were minding them. There must have been 5000 in it. These sheep are put in tight log holds every night to prevent the wolves from getting at them. The grass in these ravines and up the steep side hills for some distance is very good & the water is of the best & plenty. One of the ranches had a pet deer & it has followed us to camp, which is at the bottom of a steep & rocky hill close to a running spring brook & wood is quite plenty.

October 28th.

Snow fell last night to the depth of 4 inches & it's thawed but little. The country was much the same as yesterday & ranches are getting more plenty. We left the pet deer at the first ranch we came to this morning. At 1 P.M. we crossed the Dearborn River, a bright & swift stream & of good width, but not deep. We went but a short distance further when we went in camp. Here we met the stage which runs from Helny [Helena] to Ft. Benton twice a week. The country along the Dearborn River is very pretty in rocky scenery. It has very little valley & that only in places. The steep rocks run down to the very water's edge. This evening wood is rather scarce. We can see large forests up on high towering ridges, but that's little consolation.

" 29th.

Last night was very cold. We soon reached Wolf Creek this morning & this took us to the mouth of Prickly Pear Canyon, which runs through a range of mountains by this name which is 14 miles through by following the canyon. This ride through the canyon has interested me more than any one day ride this summer. There is a nice road cut through

the rocks most of the way, just above high water of the
creek, which is about 2 rods wide & deep in places & its
current is very swift. To give you a good description of the
rockwork is more than I can do. They are of a great height &
of every variety of color, & the rocks belong to all classes of
formation from the softest to the hardest. Besides, they are
throwed in such a queer shape. Instead of the veins running
horizontal, they are on an incline & in places perpendicular.
Of course this is very common in this part of the country, to
see the rock sit up in an incline position, but not in such a
short distance to see them in so many different positions &
of so many different classes.[48] This evening we are camped at
the end of the canyon at a ranch where we got beef, wood,
& hay for our horses. We met some Flathead Indians in the
canyon on their way to the Teton & other rivers to hunt this
fall. There is only now & then an Indian that has a rifle, but
all carry their bow & arrows yet. The road through the canyon was made in the year '63 & '64 during the first discovery
of gold at Helny, at a cost of 2,000,000.[49] At that time the
travel was up the Missouri to Benton & then overland through
this canyon to the diggings. The price of toll through the
canyon is 50 cts. for 2 horses & wagon & 25 cts. for a pack
animal or a rode one.

----

48. The picturesque canyon is traced by Little Prickly Pear Creek,
and constitutes a wonderland of red and green Precambrian mudstone.
For particulars of this and the volcanic formations viewed by Zimmer
north of Helena, see David Alt and Donald W. Hyndman, *Roadside
Geology of Montana* (Missoula: Mountain Press Publishing Company,
1986), 271–76.

49. The Wolf Creek Road more likely cost $2,000. For a discus-
sion of early roads around Helena, see Jon Axline, "Rutted Road Links
the Gulch and 'States'," in *More from the Quarries of Last Chance Gulch*
(Helena: Helena Independent Record, 1995), 121–24.

October 30th.

Last night was another cold one, yet the day has been quite pleasant. We followed Wolf Creek most of the day. The country is quite hilly but not stony. All of the tillable land has been taken up & the country is well settled. An hour before going in camp we passed a group of log houses called Silver City.[50] About a mile north of the town there is a range of hills where Silver mining is carried on heavy. Our camp tonight is on a stream that empties in the Missouri River. Brush wood is plenty & we are but 6 miles from Helny City.

" *31st.*

Weather the same as yesterday. We soon reached Helny City[51] this morning. It's built on both sides of a steep gully (where gold was first discovered in this part of Montana). It has some fine residences & good public buildings. It has 2 banks, courthouse house [sic], U.S. custom house, county jail, penitentiary & a female seminary. Its population is 5000. The Chinese number 1000. From Helny we took the Helny & Bozeman stage route, which runs on leaving Helny through Prickly Pear Valley, which is very wide & about 20 miles

---

50. Silver City stood northwest of Helena not far from Marysville, which became the center of a major gold strike in 1876. Merrill G. Burlingame and K. Ross Toole, *A History of Montana,* 3 vols. (New York: Lewis Historical Publishing Company, Inc., 1957), 2:208–9.

51. Helena City, or Helena, was founded as a result of gold discoveries in Last Chance Gulch in 1864. The pronunciation, "Hel-E-na," drew disfavor from its inhabitants, who opted to shift the accent to the first syllable while slurring the second, hence Zimmer's "Helny." Helena by 1870 became one of Montana's ranking communities, and it profited by its association with other booming communities to an extent that by 1875 it had become territorial capital. Roberta Carkeek Cheney, *Names on the Face of Montana: The Story of Montana's Place Names* (Missoula: Mountain Press Publishing Company, 1983), 134.

long & well watered from the hills on either side (which would be large mountains in the East). At the foot of these hills & up the ravines at short intervals, there is miners' cabins & in some places 18 or 20 may be seen in a group. The hills are covered with pine forest & the valley is well settled. We are going parallel with the Missouri. Only a range of hills prevents us from seeing it. Before going in camp we passed the trail which branches off from ours that leads to Diamond City[52] on the Missouri River, also a mining town, or rather kept up by miners. We are camped on a small stream & wood is plenty. A great deal of prospecting has been done in this creek bank, but the diggings are all deserted.

November 1st.
Weather fine & the country much the same as yesterday. Just before going in camp we crossed a small divide to get in the Missouri Valley, which is of good width, thickly settled & good soil. We are camped at the river which is full as wide here as at Benton & about as deep, but it's full of steep rapids & unsafe to ford, so some enterprising chap has a ferry here who does good business. On this side, a few miles below, there is a large flour mill run by the river.

" 2nd.
Weather fine. The road soon left the river & took across a mountain for short. We passed a mining town at the foothills

---

52. Diamond City was one of the anchor communities of the gold-producing Confederate Gulch that was extensively mined in 1864–68. Ibid., 73; Jean Davis, comp., *Shallow Diggin's: Tales from Montana's Ghost Towns* (Caldwell, Idaho: The Caxton Printers, Ltd., 1962), 231–37; Burlingame and Toole, *History of Montana*, 2:206.

called Hogum,[53] & on the other side another called Radersburg[54] & two others I did not learn the names. After crossing this range the country is gravelly & hilly & mines are very plenty. Water to work them is brought from the mountain in ditches & in places plank troughs, some of which are miles in length. A few miles of this & we came in a poor gravelly prairie where we camped at a spring close to the road. The water is good, but it's luke-warm. Quite a number of our wagons are empty now & we keep them to haul wood along. Only for us filling them in the mountains, we would have been out of luck for some tonight.

November 3rd.

Weather cloudy & cold. The country is some better than yesterday. We saw the Missouri several times but at a great distance. We crossed the Jefferson & Madison rivers at Gallatin City, where these 2 rivers run into the Gallatin, & from here it's called the Missouri. (So I can say that I've been at the headwaters of the Missouri as well as many other rivers in this & Dakota Ter'y.) Gallatin City[55] is a

---

53. This was Hog-Em, a mining camp so dubbed by frustrated miners who found all area pay claims "hogged up" by a few individuals. Cheney, *Names on the Face of Montana*, 138.

54. Radersburg, situated at the foot of the Elkhorn Mountains, owed its fame to the fact that the first piece of free-milling gold was found there in the early 1860s. Late in the decade, placer gold was discovered at Radersburg and in 1879 the town's population stood at 250, thereafter dropping off drastically as gold production waned. Cheney, *Names on the Face of Montana*, 218; Burlingame and Toole, *History of Montana*, 2:206; Don C. Miller, *Ghost Towns of Montana* (Boulder, Colo.: Pruett Publishing Company, 1974), 119–20.

55. Gallatin City, incorporated in 1865 following its boom, aspired to be the head of navigation on the Missouri River, but failed before realization of that destiny. By 1876, according to First Lieutenant James H. Bradley, the community consisted of but a "few straggling houses." Davis, *Shallow Diggin's*, 354.

small town of about 200 inhabitants, or rather people. From here we went up the Gallatin River a few miles & went in camp on its bank. Wood is plenty. About 200 yards from the river there is a large spring coming out from under a limestone bluff. It throws out a stream as large around as a barrel. The Gallatin Valley is very rich here, but not wide, well settled & they raise a great many black hogs. They are fatted altogether on peas which grow better than corn. (The largest patch of corn I've seen out here didn't exceed 2 acres. I guess they get too much soft corn. But let you ask them if they can raise corn, it's "Oh, yes.")

November 4th.

Two inches of snow fell last night. The day has been very pleasant & tonight it's nearly all gone. About noon we crossed the Gallatin River. The country has been very fine & we passed many good farm[s] & cattle ranch[es]. It's a low prairie & starts from the river edge & runs back for several miles on the side we were on this forenoon, but on the other broken hills come down to the riverbank, & this afternoon it's vicissitude. We went but a short distance further & went in camp on Middle Creek. We brought wood, for there is none here as most everyone knew. It's only 11 miles to Ft. Ellis now. Only for it's being Sunday I think we would have made it today.

" 5th.

Weather cool. When we were within two miles of Bozeman we were met by the Bozeman Brass Band & some ladies & gentlemen in carriages & buggies who escorted us all the way to the fort, the band playing at intervals tunes to suit the times, such as, "Johnny Has a Shot in His Leg," "The

Girl I Left Behind," &c., &c.[56] But I don't think many left girls behind them at Ft. Ellis or Bozeman, for what there is at both places would not supply one-tenth part of us. We reached Fort Ellis at 10 A.M. & found a good dinner waiting, such a one as we didn't get often the last 8 months. It was quite a surprise party to our stomachs, but they took it all in good humor. The second of March, when we left this fort, there was 90 men of us & 100 horses. Today there is but 50 horses (& some of them as unfit to ride. One of ours dropped dead just the other side of Bozeman this morning.) & 58 men returned sound & well. Two were killed. Some were wounded & left along the route along with a large number of sick. 10 have been discharged, their time being out. I think our co. used up a horse to a man, on the average. Of course, some brought the same horse in that they took out, while others used up 3 & 4. (I brought my horse in looking nearly as well as when he went out. There has been times this summer when he was poorer in flesh than now.) Other cos. of our battalion can be rated as ours, except G Co. I don't think they brought in over 30 horses.

November 6th.
Weather disagreeable. It either rained or snowed all day. S. Freer[57] of G Co. while drunk shot at one of his comrades

---

56. These were typical military songs of the day. "The Girl I Left Behind Me" was an old favorite from the Civil War. Of British origin, it was also known as "Brighton Camp" when it first appeared in print in 1808. "Johnny Has a Shot in His Leg" is perhaps an alternate or parody title for "Johnny Get Your Gun," a song known as early as the 1850s though not copyrighted in the United States until 1886. Roger Lax and Frederick Smith, *The Great Song Thesaurus* (New York: Oxford University Press, 1989), 242, 291.

57. Private Thomas Freer was from Boston, Massachusetts, and had enlisted in the army on September 11, 1876. Muster Roll, Company G, Second Cavalry, June 30–August 31, 1877, RG 94, RAMR, NA.

in the quarters, then reloaded his carbine & ran down to the brook (that supplies the fort with water) and shot himself through the left lung. He is in a low state this evening.

" *7th.*

Weather mild & very soft underfoot. At 2 A.M. Flannigan[58] of L Co. while on guard shot himself through the left hand carelessly. He had but 15 days to serve. This morning is the first that any of F, H or G Cos. went on guard. L Co. of our battalion got in fort a month before we did, & G Co. of the 7th Infantry were in here all summer, that is, the most of them. Our duty outside of guard (which comes in turn, once in 10 days) is to [go to] the stables in the morning at 7, feed and groom our horses, which takes us until 8. At 10 each man rides his horse to water which takes half an hour. Then there's no more until half past 3 P.M. The horses are rode to water, fed & groomed. This takes one & a quarter hour, then there's nothing more to do until the morrow. Oh, I forgot to mention one of our most important duties, & that is to get our 3 square meals a day which we never go back on. Our gardener raised 1500 bushels of potatoes & about the same number cabbage heads, besides carrots, onions & rutabagas by the hundreds of bushels & they are all nicely stored away in 2 underground cellars. So what the government allows us outside of this (for it has nothing to do with what we raise) we can live like kings while we are in the fort.[59]

---

58. Private John Flanagan was from Philadelphia, Pennsylvania, and was in his second enlistment. He initially enlisted on November 20, 1872. Ibid.

59. For detailed examples of daily routine at western army posts, including the maintenance of post gardens, see Rickey, *Forty Miles a Day*, 88–115.

November 8th.

Weather mild. Everything quiet, nothing going on only our regular daily duty. After this is done the time is chiefly spent in the library, which is filled with good books & papers from all parts of the states and territories.

November 9th.

Weather mild. Nothing worthy of mentioning.

" 10th.

Weather mild. The quartermaster has an auction sale of our played out horses in his corral this afternoon. Lieut. Doane of G Co. & a small party started for Tongue River to bring up some property belonging to our battalion.

" 11th.

Weather mild. This is Sunday & of course inspection comes without fail. This is the worst day in the week. Everything has to shine like a new silver dollar. If it don't, you go to the mill. (That's what the boys call the guard house, and there you have to work, such as saw wood for the officers, haul water & keep the sidewalk free from snow. But then, when you are there you have one consolation. There's a guard with you with a loaded carbine to keep off mad dogs, & at night you are locked up so there's no danger of your being stolen.)

" 12th.

Weather mild. Nothing of importance.

" 13th.

Weather mild. We drew clothing, or those that wanted.

" *14th.*

Weather cloudy. Nothing of importance.

" *15th.*

Weather cool & cloudy. We received 2 months pay this afternoon. Gambling & drinking is going quite lively. Quite a number of the boys have hung their caps up in the mill.

" *16th.*

Weather as yesterday. Private Henry Hin[e]line of our co. received his discharge on the minors act.[60]

" *17th.*

Last evening it commenced to snow. This morning it was all rain. Towards evening it commenced snowing again. In the hills or mountains, by which we are on 3 sides surrounded, it has been snowing for the last 24 hours.

November 18th.

Weather cloudy & very sloppy under foot. Sunday inspection as usual. Sergeant A. B. Conklin[61] of our co.

---

60. Corporal John H. Hineline had enlisted on September 20, 1876, in Toledo, Ohio, apparently under age twenty-one and without his parents' permission. Muster Roll, Company F, Second Cavalry, June 30–August 31, 1877. RG 94, RAMR, NA. He was dismissed on authority of Special Order 197, Adjutant General's Office. Regimental Returns of the Second Cavalry, Return for November, 1877, NAMP M744, Roll 166. The act of May 15, 1872, allowed that "no person under the age of twenty-one years shall be enlisted in the military service of the United States without the written consent of his parents or guardians." *The Military Laws of the United States*, 4th ed. (Washington, D.C.: Government Printing Office, 1908), paragraph 672.

61. Sergeant Ausburn B. Conklin had been promoted from corporal in July. He had enlisted on November 21, 1872, in New York City. Muster Roll, Company F, Second Cavalry, June 30–August 31, 1877, RG 94, RAMR, NA.

received his discharge this morning, his time being out.

" *19th.*
Weather mild. Received a pass & went to Bozeman.

" *20th.*
Weather cold. Last night 4 inches of snow fell. Sleighing is good. Sealskin caps & gloves were issued our co. this evening. (When they become worn badly you can get them exchanged, but if you have lost or sold them 5 dollars is kept out of your pay for either article.)

" *21st.*
A beautiful winter day. Just cold enough not to thaw. One of the party that are burning lime in Bear Canyon 3 miles from the fort says snow is 2 feet deep out there.[62] Private Childris[63] of our co. was this morning discharged, his time being out.

" *22nd.*
Weather mild, thawing a little.

" *23rd.*
Some snow fell last night & more during the day. It's growing very cold this evening.

---

62. Lime would have been burned to prepare it for making gesso or plaster for the various quarters of the post.

63. This is Private Marion Childers, from Louisville, Kentucky, who had enlisted on November 30, 1872. Muster Roll, Company F, Second Cavalry, June 30–August 31, 1877, RG 94, RAMR, NA.

" *24th.*

Weather nice. Fine sleighing. 4 of our men, with some others, have returned from Tongue River Post, that were left there sick in September. They say that the Yellowstone Valley is being settled up fast, that from 12 to 15 miles apart on either side of the river one can see cabins & some very good houses in the Fort Pease bottom & at Baker's battleground there is saw mills & a goodly number of houses. Also, across from the mouth of the Big Horn River there is a town starting.[64] These men say that during October hundreds of miners were coming out of the Wolf & Big Horn mountains saying that it didn't pay there to mine it in a small way. Gold wasn't plenty enough. Those that came from the Wolf Mountains down Tongue River or the Rosebud say that if these streams were turned and the beds were worked that it would be a paying speck. Most of these miners were formerly from the Black Hills. They had got disgusted

---

64. This was either Pease City, established near the site of the former trading post of Fort Pease, abandoned since early 1876, or Terry's Landing. "Pease City," wrote a contemporary observer, "situated about 2 miles below the mouth of the Bighorn, is composed of two log huts, an exceedingly small 'block house,' a small corral, and a vegetable garden in which was seen growing a fine promise of potatoes, corn, cabbage, and oats." "Copy of Memoranda made by O. M. Poe, Colonel, A.D.C., etc., while Accompanying General W. T. Sherman on a Trip from the Mississippi River to the Pacific Ocean, during the Months of July, August, September, and October, 1877," in *Reports of Inspection Made in the Summer of 1877 by Generals P. H. Sheridan and W. T. Sherman of Country North of the Union Pacific Railroad* (1878; reprint, Fairfield, Washington: Ye Galleon Press, 1984), 88. Terry's Landing, founded in June 1877, on the north side of the Yellowstone above the confluence of the Bighorn, was opposite Cantonment Terry and catered to the soldiers posted there. It soon boasted saloons, a dance house, and a restaurant, and eventually changed its name to Junction City. Topping, *Chronicles of the Yellowstone*, 231.

with the small yield, so they are a-going to try the Montana mines.[65]

November 25th.
The wind blew very hard last night & it's kept up nearly all day. Another Sunday inspection.

" *26th.*
Weather fair. We had a little snow fall last night. At 2 P.M. a detachment of G Co. 7th Inft. returned. They were in the Missoula Valley this fall while some contractors were putting up some barracks for 2 cos. of infantry who are to be stationed there hereafter. G Co. of the 7th Inft. lost 14 out of 25 of their men that were with Col. Gibbon at the Deer Lodge fight with the Nez Perces.[66]

" *27th.*
Weather fair & sleighing splendid. The officers & their ladies are spinning around the block lively.

" *28th.*
Weather cold. Capt. George L. Tyler[67] of our co. left this evening on a one-year's leave of absence. Now our co. has no commissioned officers. First Lieut. Grugan[68] I never saw.

---

65. The promise of Montana gold attracted many miners from the Black Hills diggings between 1876 and 1879. The "Big Horn stampede" was one of several small rushes that drew prospectors into the area. Parker, *Gold in the Black Hills*, 102.

66. The reference is to the Battle of the Big Hole, August 9–10, 1877. See part 2, footnote 12.

67. For a biographical sketch of Tyler, see part 1, footnote 6.

68. Frank Carter Grugan (1842–1917), from Pennsylvania and a veteran of Civil War battles in the Virginia theater at the Wilderness,

He is on the weather signal service somewhere east. Sec. Lieut. Fuller[69] got wounded in the Muddy Creek fight & he has not returned off of his sick leave of 8 months. So at the present First Lieut. Hamilton[70] of L Co. is in charge.

November 29th.

Weather mild. Thanksgiving & the men in general are filling up with good things. This evening there is to be a grand ball in the theater building.

" 30th.

Weather splendid, just cold enough not to thaw. The ball last night was a grand success. Officers & men, all dressed in their dark blue fan-tailed dress coats with buff-colored trimming hard to be sneezed at and can't be seen at will. The supper was a very good one considering everything was cold except coffee, tea & chocolate. Corporal Jones[71] was made sergeant this

---

Spotsylvania, Cold Harbor, and Petersburg, among others, joined the Second Cavalry as second lieutenant in 1866. Promoted first lieutenant in the following year, Grugan saw action against the Teton Sioux Indians during the Yellowstone Expedition of 1873, but from then until 1879 he was detailed to the Signal Office. Thereafter transferring to the Second Artillery, Grugan advanced to captain in 1885 and retired from the army in 1899. Hamersly, *Records of Living Officers*, 205; Carroll and Price, *Roll Call on the Little Big Horn*, 131.

69. For a biographical sketch of Fuller, see part 1, footnote 32.

70. Samuel Todd Hamilton (1844–1906), a Pennsylvanian, served in state regiments as an enlisted man during the Civil War. Commissioned in the Second Cavalry in 1866, Hamilton won promotion to first lieutenant in 1867. Promoted captain in 1879, he retired in 1892. Carroll and Price, *Roll Call on the Little Big Horn*, 132.

71. John W. Jones enlisted in St. Louis on July 1, 1875. He was appointed sergeant under Special Order No. 80, Headquarters, Second Cavalry. Muster Roll, Company F, Second Cavalry, June 30–August 31, 1877, RG 94, RAMR, NA.

evening in Sergeant Conklin's place (discharged), and Private Glesner[72] was made corporal in Jones's place.

December 1st.
Weather mild.

" *2nd.*
Weather mild. Sunday inspection as usual.

" *3rd.*
Weather cold.

" *4th.*
Weather cold & stormy. A small party started for Tongue River this afternoon with a poor herd of mules.

" *5th.*
Weather cold. One sergeant & 3 men all of our co. went on a 10 days' hunt along the upper part of Shields River. (I hope they will have luck. I would like a piece of deer or antelope steak.)

" *6th.*
More snow last night & today the weather is thawing. An order has been issued that the cos. horses shall be rode one hour each day for exercise if the weather permits.

December 7th.
Weather quite warm & the snow is disappearing quite fast.

---

72. This is Phillippi Glesener, who had enlisted on September 21, 1876, in New York City. Ibid.

" *8th.*

A little snow fell last night and today it's warm & thawing rapidly.

" *9th.*

The sun came out so strong today that it's left no snow on the beaten roads by this evening. (Sunday inspection.) The party that started for Tongue Riv a few days ago returned this evening with the mules. They found the snow so deep generally that the mules couldn't get enough to live on & they were in a poor condition on the start. They got no further than the mouth of Shields River before they commenced to play out.

" *10th.*

Weather warm & sloppy under foot.

" *11th.*

Weather as yesterday. A ten–horse–power circular saw was set up today so that the prisoners can saw wood for the whole garrison.

" *12th.*

Weather cooler. Our men returned off of their hunting trip. They brought as much as their team could bring besides their own camping outfit, the snow being very deep in the hills. They brought 2 large elk & 3 large deer. The largest elk weighed 800 lbs. While exercising today, Comstock[73] of our co. got thrown off his horse & broke a

---

73. Private Hugh D. Comstock had enlisted on September 11, 1876, in Buffalo, New York. Ibid.

collar bone. I finished a volume entitled *Around the World in 80 Days*, author, Jules Verne (very good).[74]

" *13th.*
Weather as yesterday. We had roast elk for dinner today. It was superior to good beef.

December 14th.
Weather very mild. Orders have been given for companies to have target practice once a week. Our co. had their's today.[75]

" *15th.*
Weather mild. Our dining room pantry has been supplied with a new supply of Centennial china ware.[76]

" *16th.*
Weather mild. Sunday inspection as usual.

" *17th.*
Weather continues mild, thawing days & freezing nights. Finished the volume entitled *The Old-Fashioned Girl* (author Mrs. Alcott. Good.)[77]

---

74. Several English editions of Verne's *Around the World in Eighty Days* were published between 1872 and 1876; an edition published by Boston's Osgood firm appeared in 1873 and 1874.

75. For a discussion of army marksmanship training during the Indian wars period, see McChristian, *An Army of Marksmen.*

76. Zimmer is likely referring to one of several china patterns manufactured in Great Britain and the United States to commemorate the centennial of American independence.

77. Editions of Louisa M. Alcott's *An Old-Fashioned Girl* were published by the Boston firm of Roberts Brothers in 1870 and 1874.

" *18th.*
Weather as yesterday.

" *19th.*
Weather cooler. This morning a detail started again for Tongue River with those mules, this time taking some wagons & oats. Finished a pamphlet entitled *Quiet Miss Godolphin* (by Ruth Garrett. Is good.)[78]

" *20th.*
Weather as yesterday. A farmer brought us 35 chickens to start Christmas dinner with.

" *21st.*
Weather cooler than herebefore, & this evening 3 inches of snow fell.

" *22nd.*
Weather still cold. Finished reading a volume entitled *Twenty Thousand Leagues under the Sea* (author Jules Verne). Very good, a scientific fiction.[79]

" *23rd.*
Weather cold & sleighing good. Sunday inspection as usual. It comes as regular as time.

---

78. *Quiet Miss Godolphin*, a novelette of 110 pages authored by Mrs. Isabella Mayo, was published in 1871 in Philadelphia by J. B. Lippincott and Company. Ruth Garrett was possibly a pen name of the author.

79. Jules Verne, *Twenty Thousand Leagues under the Sea*, was translated from the French and published in London in 1873 and 1876 and in Chicago in 1876.

" *24th.*

Weather cold. H Co. is having a dance in their quarters this evening.

December 25th.

Weather cold. (Another Christmas rolls over our heads & another year older but still wiser.) The cos. in general are having nice dinners. Ours especially had as nice a dinner as money can procure. Finished the reading of a volume of stories entitled *Cloudy Pictures*, a translation from German (by F. H. Underwood).[80]

" *26th.*

The weather is the same as it's been for the last week. We had target practice again today.

" *27th.*

Weather the same. R. M. Jones[81] of our co. was discharged this morning, cause disability.

" *28th.*

Had a little snow fall last night which has improved the sleighing. This evening we received 35 volumes of the latest novels by the best authors.

---

80. Zimmer refers to Francis H. Underwood, *Cloud-Pictures*, published in Boston by Lee and Shepard, 1872, and in New York by Lee, Shepard, and Dillingham in the same year. The volume embraced four stories of German origin: "The Exile of von Adelstein's Soul," "Topankalon," "Herr Regenbogen's Concert," and "A Great-Organ Prelude."

81. Private Riley M. Jones had enlisted on August 22, 1876, at St. Louis, Missouri. Muster Roll, Company F, Second Cavalry, June 30–August 31, 1877, RG 94, RAMR, NA.

" *29th.*

Weather cold & a little more snow last night.

" *30th.*

Weather cold. Last night was the coldest night we have had this winter. Sunday inspection. Nothing else of importance.

" *31st.*

Still cold. Last night the thermometer went down to zero. We were mustered for two months pay this morning. Many a good resolution has been passed this evening on the Old Year's going out by the boys, only to be broken the next pay day. Finished reading the volume *It's Never Too Late to Mend* (by Charles Reade. Very good.)[82]

---

82. Popular novelist Reade's *It Is Never Too Late to Mend: A Matter-of-Fact Romance*, first published in Boston in 1872, also appeared in editions published by Harper and Brothers, New York, in 1876 and 1877.

Postscript

On November 8, 1877, three days after the Montana Battalion of the Second Cavalry had returned to its home station at Fort Ellis, the *Bozeman Times* editorialized about the troops' eventful duty "abroad."

Three Companies of the 2d Cavalry, F, H, and G, in command of Captain Tyler, passed through town Monday, on their return to Fort Ellis. They left Fort Ellis on the 24th of March last, and had been gone nearly eight months. They were in the Muddy Creek fight; also in the fight with Joseph and the Nez Perces, at Bear Paw Mountain [sic], where that chief was captured. They suffered many privations, living on nothing for three days while fighting Joseph and his band. They have the true grit, having distinguished themselves in every engagement. They were met about a mile from town by a number of citizens and the Bozeman Silver Cornet Band, and escorted through Bozeman to Fort Ellis. These soldiers, although cov-

ered with dust and browned by exposure in their long
march from the scene of their recent conflict, presented
a fine appearance. The horses looked somewhat jaded
and fatigued, but will now have a chance to recuperate, as
the fall campaign has ended, and the soldiers gone into
winter quarters at Fort Ellis. A great work has been ac-
complished, in capturing the hostile Nez Perces and pre-
venting an alliance with Sitting Bull, which doubtless
would have been the cause of trouble on the northern
border of Montana, as it is often difficult to know what
band or tribe of Indians to attribute robberies and mur-
ders to. Too much praise cannot be placed to the credit of
Gen. Miles and the officers and men who crushed out
the power of the Nez Perces to do evil.

The performance of the Montana Battalion during the
Sioux and Nez Perce campaigns also prompted the fol-
lowing recognition, as published in the *Bozeman Times*,
November 8, 1877:

Hdq's Dist. of the Yellowstone, Cantonment at Tongue
River, M.T., October 16, 1877.
Com'dg Officer (Battalion 2d Cav.):

Sir:—I have the honor to communicate to you the
following by direction of the Commanding Officer:
In reviewing the Battalion, 2d Cavalry, the Commanding Officer is pleased to acknowledge its valuable service
during the Spring and Summer operations against hostile
Indians. Equally on the most fatiguing march in pursuit of
fleeing Indians, as in action, you have displayed those qualities most commendable to the American soldier; and you
will please convey to the officers and men of the Battalion,

his sincere appreciation of the same, and express to them his regrets at being obliged to part with a command whose faithful performance of all duties he could so truly rely upon.

Very Respectfully,
Your ob't servant,
FRANK D. BALDWIN,
1st Lieut. 5th Inf'ty, A.D.C.[1]

---

1. Frank D. Baldwin (1842–1923) served as Miles's adjutant during much of the Indian campaigning on the northern plains in 1876 and 1877. A Michigan native, he had enlisted in the Michigan Horse Guards in 1861, but served as an officer in his state's infantry volunteers through the balance of the Civil War. Joining the Fifth Infantry in 1869, Baldwin fought in the Red River War of 1874–75 and in the Great Sioux War of 1876–77. (Years later he would receive two Medals of Honor—one for "distinguished bravery" during his Civil War Service at Peach Tree Creek, Georgia, in 1864, and another for gallantry in battling Cheyennes at McClellan's Creek, Texas, in which engagement his troops rescued two white women captives. He also received brevet promotions for his various Indian service. Baldwin later served in the Philippines and retired a brigadier general in 1906. His biography is in Robert H. Steinbach, *A Long March: The Lives of Frank and Alice Baldwin* (Austin: University of Texas Press, 1989). For a brief treatment, see Robert C. Carriker, "Frank D. Baldwin," in Paul A. Hutton, *Soldiers West: Biographies from the Military Frontier* (Lincoln: University of Nebraska Press, 1987), 228-42. See also, Heitman, *Historical Register*, 1:185-86.

Index